Simon Stephens

Wastwater

and

T5

Methuen Drama

Published by Methuen Drama 2011

Methuen Drama, an imprint of Bloomsbury Publishing Plc

1 3 5 7 9 10 8 6 4 2

Methuen Drama
Bloomsbury Publishing Plc
36 Soho Square
London W1D 3QY
www.methuendrama.com

First published by Methuen Drama in 2011

ISBN: 978 1 408 15486 1

A CIP catalogue record for this book is available from
the British Library

Available in the USA from Bloomsbury Academic & Professional,
175 Fifth Avenue/3rd Floor, New York, NY 10010.
www.BloomsburyAcademicUSA.com

Typeset by Country Setting, Kingsdown, Kent
Printed and bound in Great Britain by
CPI Cox & Wyman Ltd, Reading, Berkshire

ROYAL COURT

The Royal Court Theatre presents

WASTWATER

by **Simon Stephens**

First performance at the Royal Court Jerwood Theatre Downstairs, Sloane Square, London on Thursday 31 March 2011.

First performance at the Wiener Festwochen, Halle G in MuseumsQuartier, Vienna on Saturday 14 May 2011.

WASTWATER is a co-production with the Wiener Festwochen (Vienna).

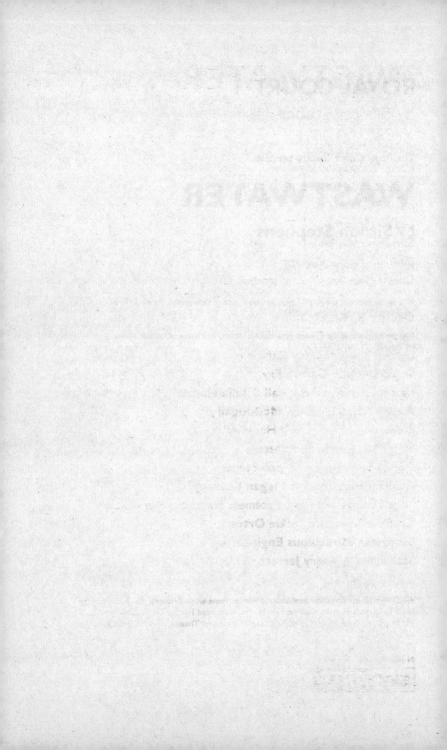

WASTWATER

by Simon Stephens

in order of appearance

Harry **Tom Sturridge**

Frieda **Linda Bassett**

Mark **Paul Ready**

Lisa **Jo McInnes**

Sian **Amanda Hale**

Jonathan **Angus Wright**

Dalisay **Jasmine Chen, Candice Chen**

Director **Katie Mitchell**

Designer **Lizzie Clachan**

Lighting Designer **Lucy Carter**

Sound Designer **Gareth Fry**

Casting Directors **Amy Ball & Julia Horan**

Assistant Director **Ellen McDougall**

Production Manager **Paul Handley**

Stage Manager **Michael Dennis**

Deputy Stage Manager **Pippa Meyer**

Assistant Stage Manager **Megan Kearney**

Stage Management Work Placement **Natascha Kurzreiter**

Costume Supervisor **Jackie Orton**

Set built by **Miraculous Engineering**

Set painted by **Kerry Jarrett**

The Royal Court Theatre and Stage Management wish to thank the following for their help with this production: Keir Bosley, Hampstead Theatre, Lyric Hammersmith, MacKing.co.uk, Peter Jones, RADA, Regent's Park Open Air Theatre, Young Vic Theatre.

Media Partner

THE COMPANY

SIMON STEPHENS (Writer)

FOR THE ROYAL COURT: Motortown, Country Music, Herons, Bluebird.

OTHER THEATRE INCLUDES: Punk Rock (Lyric Hammersmith/Manchester Royal Exchange); Marine Parade (Brighton Festival); A Thousand Stars Explode in the Sky (Lyric Hammersmith); The Trial of Ubu (Schauspielhaus, Essen/Toneelgroep, Amsterdam); Pornography (Tricycle/Birmingham Rep/Traverse/Deutsches Schauspielhaus, Hanover); Sea Wall (Bush/Traverse); Harper Regan (National); On the Shore of the Wide World (National/Manchester Royal Exchange); Port (Manchester Royal Exchange).

TV INCLUDES: Dive, Pornography.

AWARDS: 2005 Olivier Best New Play award for On the Shore of the Wide World, 2002 Pearson Award, Best New Play for Port.

LINDA BASSETT (Frieda)

FOR THE ROYAL COURT: The Stone, Lucky Dog, Far Away (& Albery), The Recruiting Officer, Our Country's Good, Serious Money (& Wyndhams & Public Theatre, New York); East Is East (with Tamasha Theatre Company & Birmingham Rep & Theatre Royal Stratford East/Duke of York's); Aunt Dan & Lemon (& Public Theatre, New York), Abel's Sister, Fen (with Joint Stock/Public Theatre, New York).

OTHER THEATRE INCLUDES: The Road to Mecca (Arcola); A Winter's Tale, Pericles, Henry IV Part I & II, The Theban Plays, Artists & Admirers (RSC); Phaedra (Donmar); Hortensia and The Museum of Dreams (Finborough); Love Me Tonight, Out in the Open, The Awakening (Hampstead); Richard III, Taming of the Shrew (Globe) John Gabriel Borkman (English Touring Co); Five Kinds of Silence (Lyric Hammersmith); The Triumph of Love (Almeida/UK Tour); The Clearing (Bush); Schism in England, Juno & The Paycock, A Place with the Pigs (National); The Seagull (Liverpool Playhouse); Medea, The Bald Prima Donna (Leicester Haymarket/Liverpool Playhouse/Almeida); The Cherry Orchard (Leicester Haymarket); Falkland Sound/Voces de Malvinas (Belgrade T.I.E team/Interplay Leeds/Coventry).

TV INCLUDES: Grandma's House, Lark Rise to Candleford, Sense and Sensibility, The Brief, This Little Life, Our Mutual Friend, Far from the Madding Crowd, Silent Film, Christmas, A Small Dance, No Bananas, Newshounds, Bramwell, Loved Up, Skallagrig.

FILM INCLUDES: West is West, The Reader, Separate Lies, Calendar Girls, The Hours, The Martins, East is East, Beautiful People, Oscar &Lucinda, Mary Reilly, Waiting for the Moon.

AWARDS INCLUDE: 2004 TMA Best Actress Award for Lucky Dog, 2001 Clarence Derwent Best Actess in a Supporting Role Award for Far Away, Best Actress Award Semana Internacional de Cine Valladolid Espania for East is East.

LUCY CARTER (Lighting Designer)

PREVIOUSLY WITH KATIE MITCHELL: Parthenogenisis (ROH)

THEATRE INCLUDES: Breathing Irregular (Gate); Where there's a Will (ETT); The Crucible (Abbey, Dublin); The Fourth Wiseman (The Arc, Dublin); Wonderful Tennessee (Lyric, Belfast); Kirikou and Karaba (LLO Music, France).

RECENT WORK WITH CHOREOGRAPHER WAYNE McGREGOR: FAR (Random); Chroma (San Francisco Ballet/National Ballet of Canada/Royal Ballet/Bolshoi); L'Anatomie de la Sensation (Paris Opera Ballet); Dyad 1909 (Random & Sadlers Wells); Dyad 1929 (Australian Ballet); Yantra (Stuttgart Ballet); Outlier (New York City Ballet); Limen, Infra, Qualia (Royal Ballet); Genus (Paris Opera Ballet); Skindex, Renature (Nederlands Dans Theater); Entity, Amu, Digit01, Ataxia, Nemesis, Erazor (Random); 2 Human (English National Ballet); Nautilus (Stuttgart).

OTHER DANCE INCLUDES: The Most Incredible Thing (Sadlers Wells); Still Life (Val Caniparoli/ Scottish Ballet); Invitus Invitam (Kim Brandstrup/Royal Ballet); The Two of Us, Silence of the Soul, 5 2 10 (WDPM); Reflections (Rambert); Snow White in Black (Phoenix); Just Add Water, Exit no Exit, Faultline (Shobana Jeyasingh); When Once is Never Enough, Faun, As You Are (Cois Ceim).

OPERA INCLUDES: Maria Stuarda (Opera North); The Adventures of Mr Broucek (Opera North/Scottish Opera); Dido and Aeneas, Acis and Galatea (ROH/Royal Ballet); Imeneo (Opera Ireland).

AWARDS: 2008 Knight of Illumination Award for Dance, Chroma 2008.

CANDICE CHEN (Dalisay)

THEATRE INCLUDES: The King and I (Raymond Gubbay Ltd).

JASMINE CHEN (Dalisay)

Jasmine is making her professional stage debut in Wastwater.

FILM INCLUDES: Harry Potter and the Deathly Hallows.

LIZZIE CLACHAN (Designer)

FOR THE ROYAL COURT: Our Private Life, Aunt Dan and Lemon, The Girlfriend Experience (& Plymouth Drum); On Insomnia and Midnight (Festival Internacional Cervantino, Guanajuato & Centro Cultural Helénico, Mexico City); Woman and Scarecrow, Ladybird.

OTHER THEATRE/OPERA INCLUDES: Tiger Country (Hampstead); Far Away (Bristol Old Vic); Bliss (Staatsoper, Hamburg); Treasure Island (West End); Shoot/Get Treasure/Repeat (Paines Plough); Contains Violence, Absolute Beginners (Hammersmith Lyric); Money, Tropicana (Shunt/National); Amato Saltone, Dance Bear Dance, The Ballad of Bobby François, The Tennis Show (Shunt); Soldier's Fortune (Young Vic); Bedtime Story & The End of the Beginning (Union Theatre/Young Vic); Julie, Gobbo (National Theatre of Scotland); Factory Girls (Arcola); Ether Frolics (Shunt/Sound & Fury); I'll Be The Devil, Days of Significance, The American Pilot (RSC); All in the Timing (Peepolykus national tour); Moonstone (Royal Exchange).

Lizzie co-founded Shunt in 1998 and is an Artistic Director of the company.

GARETH FRY (Sound Designer)

FOR THE ROYAL COURT: Sucker Punch, The City, O Go My Man (with Out of Joint); Talking to Terrorists (with Out of Joint); Harvest, Forty Winks, Under the Whaleback, Night Songs, Face to the Wall, Redundant, Mountain Language/Ashes to Ashes, The Country.

OTHER THEATRE INCLUDES: Black Watch, Peter Pan, Be Near Me (National Theatre of Scotland); Joe Turner's Come and Gone, Sweet Nothings, The Jewish Wife (Young Vic); Babel (Stan Won't Dance); No Idea (Improbable); The Prisoner of 2nd Avenue (Vaudeville Theatre); Light Shining in Buckinghamshire (Arcola); Fraulein Julie (Schabühne, Berlin); The Duchess of Malfi (Northampton); Beauty and the Beast (Cottesloe Theatre); Endgame, Shun-kin (Complicité); Noise of Time (Complicité with th Emerson String Quartet); Othello (Frantic Assembly); The Fahrenheit Twins (Told By An Idiot); Tangle, Zero Degrees and Drifting (Unlimited Theatre); Astronaut (Theatre O); The Bull, The Flowerbed, Giselle (Fabulous Beast Dance Theatre at the Barbican); Living Costs (DV8 at Tate Modern); After Dido (ENO); Dancing at Lughnasa (Old Vic); Shadowmouth, Romans in Britain (Sheffield Crucible); Phaedra's Love (Bristol Old Vic & Barbican); The Watery Part of the World (Sound & Fury, BAC & UK tour); The Cat in the Hat, Pains of Youth, Some Trace Of Her, Fram, Women of Troy, Kneehigh's A Matter Of Life and Death, Attempts on Her Life, Waves, The Overwhelming, Improbable's Theatre of Blood, Fix Up, Iphigenia at Aulis, The Three Sisters, Ivanov, The Oresteia (National); The Overwhelming (Laura Pels Theatre, NY); Macbeth (Out of Joint).

RADIO INCLUDES: Jump, OK Computer, The Overwhelming (BBC Radio)

EVENTS INCLUDE: Somerset House Film4 Summer Screen & Ice Rink, Pixar's The Big Cheese tour.

AWARDS INCLUDE: Laurence Olivier Award 2007 for Waves; Helpmann Award 2008 for Black Watch; Olivier Award 2009 for Black Watch.

AMANDA HALE (Sian)

FOR THE ROYAL COURT: The City.

OTHER THEATRE INCLUDES: Elektra, After Dido, King Lear (Young Vic); Our Class (National); Pornography (Birmingham Rep/Traverse/Tricycle); The Glass Menagerie (Bill Kenwright Productions); Crooked (Bush); The Importance of Being Earnest (Oxford Playhouse).

TELEVSION INCLUDES: Crimson Petal and the White, Any Human Heart, Spooks, Murderland, Persuasion, Richard is My Boyfriend.

ELLEN McDOUGALL (Assistant Director)

AS DIRECTOR: Ivan and the Dogs (ATC/Soho); (I'm in) Brooklyn (not Dagenham Parkway) (Miniaturists, Arcola); Am I Comforting You Now? (Company of Angels, Theatre Cafe 2010); St Kilda (a devised piece scratched at The Arches and developed at the NT Studio); The Invisible Woman (Young Vic/ATC); Tri-umph (Burton Taylor Studio); Betting on the Dust Commander (Albany Theatre Studio); Philadelphia Here I Come!, Cymbeline (Bedlam Theatre).

AS ASSISTANT DIRECTOR: Beauty and the Beast, Women Beware Women, Cat in a Hat, Our Class (National); Tunnel 228 (Punchdrunk); The Brothers Size (ATC/Young Vic).

Ellen was Director in Residence at the NT Studio 2009, and has since directed various workshops and readings there. She was awarded the Runner Up Prize in the JMK 2008 and directed a workshop on A Kind of Alaska (BAC).

Ellen is Associate Artist at ATC, and an Associate Reader at Soho Theatre

JO McINNES (Lisa)

FOR THE ROYAL COURT: Fleshwound, 4.48 Psychosis (& US tour), Bluebird.

OTHER THEATRE INCLUDES: The House of Bernarda Alba, The Children's Hour (National); M.A.D (Bush); dirty butterfly (Soho); Inland Sea (Oxford Stage Company); Edward II (Sheffield Crucible); Biloxi Blues, The Importance of Being Earnest, Wait until Dark, Memoirs of a Survivor (Salisbury Playhouse); Tess of the D'Urbavilles (Basingstoke); Uncle Vanya, The Herbal Bed, As You Like It (RSC).

TELEVISION INCLUDES: Five Daughters, Material Girl, Afterlife, Recovery, The World of Impressionists, Spooks, The Playground, Playing the Field.

FILM INCLUDES: Me and Orson Welles, Brown Paper Bag, The New Romantics, My Wife is an Actress, Birthday Girl, Gangster No. 1.

RADIO INCLUDES: The Pet, Cut Me and I Bleed Elvis, Death of an Altruist, Night on the Town, Scars, Uncertainty.

KATIE MITCHELL (Director)

FOR THE ROYAL COURT: The City, Forty Winks, Nightsongs, The Country, Live Like Pigs, Mountain Language/ Ashes to Ashes (& New York).

OTHER THEATRE INCLUDES: Beauty and the Beast, The Cat in the Hat, Pains of Youth, Some Trace of Her, Rutherford and Son, The Machine Wreckers, The Oresteia, The Three Sisters, Iphigenia at Aulis, A Dream Play, The Seagull, Waves, Attempts on her Life, Women of Troy (National); A Woman Killed with Kindness, The Dybbuk, Ghosts, Henry VI, Easter, The Phoenician Women, The Mysteries, Beckett Shorts (RSC); Uncle Vanya (RSC/Young Vic); The Last Ones, Iphigenia in Aulis (Abbey, Dublin); Endgame (Donmar); Attempts on Her Life (Piccolo Teatro, Milan); The Jewish Wife, The Maids (Young Vic); Easter, Krapp's Last Tape (Royal Dramatic Theatre, Stockholm); Request Programme (Cologne Shauspielhaus); Fräulein Julie (Schaubuhne Theatre, Berlin).

OPERA INCLUDES: Al Gran Sole Carico d'Amore (Salzburg Festival); Parthenogenesis (ROH); Idomeneo, After Dido (ENO); Don Giovanni, Jephtha, The Sacrifice, Jenufa, Katya Kabanova (Welsh National Opera); St Matthew Passion (Glyndebourne Opera).

AWARDS INCLUDE: Best Director Evening Standard Award 2006 for The Phoenician Women.

Katie is an Associate of the National.

PAUL READY (Mark)

FOR THE ROYAL COURT: Forty Winks, Terrorism, Black Milk, Crazyblackmuthafuckingself.

OTHER THEATRE INCLUDES: London Assurance, Three More Sleepless Nights, Time and the Conways, Major Barbara, Attempts on Her Life, Waves (National); Love's Labour's Lost (Shakespeare's Globe); The Pillowman (The Curve, Leicester); One Flew Over The Cuckoo's Nest (West End); Romance (Almeida); World Music (Sheffield Crucible/Donmar); Comedy of Errors (Bristol Old Vic); Romeo and Juliet (Liverpool Playhouse); Mother Clapp's Molly House (National/West End); Twelfth Night (Liverpool Playhouse & Everyman); Cuckoo's (Gate); The Beggar's Opera (Broomhill Opera at Wilton's Music Hall); Are You Ready? Yes (Bloomsbury Theatre).

TELEVISION INCLUDES: Silk, Doc Martin, Pulling, Holby City, Trial and Retribution, Twisted Tales, Born and Bred, Life Begins, Jeffrey Archer: The Truth, Heartbeat, Tipping the Velvet, Chambers, Harry Enfield Presents, Princess, Poirot, Plain Jane, The Practice.

FILM INCLUDES: Pierrepoint, Dresden, Maybe Baby, Angels and Insects.

RADIO INCLUDES: Billiards at Nine Thirty, The Girl from the Sea, Coram Boy.

TOM STURRIDGE (Harry)

THEATRE INCLUDES: Punk Rock (Lyric Hammersmith/Manchester Royal Exchange).

TELEVISION: Waste of Shame.

FILM: On the Road, Junkhearts, Waiting for Forever, The Boat That Rocked, Like Minds, Brothers of the Head, Being Julia, Vanity Fair.

AWARDS: 2010 Critics' Circle Best Newcomer award for Punk Rock, 2009 Best Newcomer award at Manchester Evening News Theatre Awards for Punk Rock.

ANGUS WRIGHT (Jonathan)

THEATRE INCLUDES: Design for Living (Old Vic); Cat in the Hat, Mrs Affleck, War Horse, St Joan, The Seagull, Mesure for Measure, A Dream Play, Stuff Happens, Three Sisters, Chips with Everything, Mother Courage (National); The Tragedy of Thomas Hobbes, The Merchant of Venice, Talk of the City, Hamlet, The Theban Plays, Henry IV Parts 1 & 2, Twelfth Night (RSC); Measure for Measure (Complicite); Twelfth Night (Shakespeare's Globe); Three Sisters (Chichester Festival Theatre); The Importance of Being Earnest (Nottingham Playhouse); A Midsummer Night's Dream (Almeida); A Mongrel's Heart, Private Lives (Royal Lyceum, Edinburgh); Salome (European tour); Too Clever by Half, Uncle Vanya (Moscow Arts Theatre School).

TELEVISION INCLUDES: The Sarah Jane Adventures, Above Suspicion, The Shooting of Thomas Hurndall, Waking the Dead, Hotel Babylon, The Last Duel, Casanova, Winter Solstice, Wire in the Blood, Boudica, Cambridge Spies, The Way We Live Now, The Vice, Whistleblower, Attachments, Brilliant, Dalziel & Pascoe, The Painted Lady, Duck Patrol, Soldier Soldier, Pie in the Sky, Crocodile Shoes, The Bill, Between the Lines.

FILM INCLUDES: The Iron Lady, The Bank Job, Kingdom of Heaven, Nicholas Nickleby, Dr Sleep, Charlotte Gray, Labyrinth, Affair of the Necklace, Bridget Jones's Diary, The Lover's Prayer, RKO 281, Jilting Joe, Cutthroat Island, First Knight, Frankenstein.

RADIO INCLUDES: The Secret Pilgrim, Plenty, Precious.

THE ENGLISH STAGE COMPANY
AT THE ROYAL COURT THEATRE

'For me the theatre is really a religion or way of life.
You must decide what you feel the world is about
and what you want to say about it, so that everything
in the theatre you work in is saying the same thing
... A theatre must have a recognisable attitude. It will
have one, whether you like it or not.'

George Devine, first artistic director of the
English Stage Company: notes for an unwritten
book.

photo: Stephen Cummiskey

As Britain's leading national company dedicated to new work, the Royal Court Theatre produces new plays of the highest quality, working with writers from all backgrounds, and asking questions about who we are and the world in which we live.

"The Royal Court has been at the centre of British cultural life for the past 50 years, an engine room for new writing and constantly transforming the theatrical culture." Stephen Daldry

Since its foundation in 1956, the Royal Court has presented premieres by almost every leading contemporary British playwright, from John Osborne's Look Back in Anger to Caryl Churchill's A Number and Tom Stoppard's Rock 'n' Roll. Just some of the other writers to have chosen the Royal Court to premiere their work include Edward Albee, John Arden, Richard Bean, Samuel Beckett, Edward Bond, Leo Butler, Jez Butterworth, Martin Crimp, Ariel Dorfman, Stella Feehily, Christopher Hampton, David Hare, Eugène Ionesco, Ann Jellicoe, Terry Johnson, Sarah Kane, David Mamet, Martin McDonagh, Conor McPherson, Joe Penhall, Lucy Prebble, Mark Ravenhill, Simon Stephens, Wole Soyinka, Polly Stenham, David Storey, Debbie Tucker Green, Arnold Wesker and Roy Williams.

"It is risky to miss a production there." Financial Times

In addition to its full-scale productions, the Royal Court also facilitates international work at a grass roots level, developing exchanges which bring young writers to Britain and sending British writers, actors and directors to work with artists around the world. The research and play development arm of the Royal Court Theatre, The Studio, finds the most exciting and diverse range of new voices in the UK. The Studio runs play-writing groups including the Young Writers Programme, Critical Mass for black, Asian and minority ethnic writers and the biennial Young Writers Festival. For further information, go to www.royalcourttheatre.com/ywp.

"Yes, the Royal Court is on a roll. Yes, Dominic Cooke has just the genius and kick that this venue needs... It's fist-bitingly exciting." Independent

MAKING IT HAPPEN

The Royal Court develops and produces more new plays than any other national theatre in the UK. To produce such a broad and eclectic programme and all of our play development activities costs over £5 million every year. Just under half of this is met by principal funding from Arts Council England. The rest must be found from box office income, trading and financial support from private individuals, companies and charitable foundations. The Royal Court is a registered charity (231242) and grateful for every donation it receives towards its work.

You can support the theatre by joining one of its membership schemes or by making a donation towards the Writers Development Fund. The Fund underpins all of the work that the Royal Court undertakes with new and emerging playwrights across the globe, giving them the tools and opportunities to flourish.

To find out how to become involved with the Royal Court and the difference that your support could make visit www.royalcourttheatre.com/support-us or call the Development Office on 020 7565 5049.

MAJOR PARTNERSHIPS

The Royal Court is able to offer its unique playwriting and audience development programmes because of significant and longstanding partnerships with the organisations that support it.

Principal funding is received from Arts Council England. The Genesis Foundation supports the Royal Court's work with International Playwrights. Theatre Local is sponsored by Bloomberg. The Jerwood Charitable Foundation supports new plays by playwrights through the Jerwood New Playwrights series. The Artistic Director's Chair is supported by a lead grant from The Peter Jay Sharp Foundation, contributing to the activities of the Artistic Director's office. Over the past ten years the BBC has supported the Gerald Chapman Fund for directors.

Sky Arts is the Media Partner for WASTWATER. In April and May, watch a documentary about the production including exclusive interviews with Simon Stephens and Katie Mitchell on Sky Arts 1 HD or you can see it online at sky.com/arts.

DEVELOPMENT ADVOCATES

John Ayton
Elizabeth Bandeen
Tim Blythe
Anthony Burton
Sindy Caplan
Cas Donald (Vice Chair)
Allie Esiri
Celeste Fenichel
Anoushka Healy
Emma Marsh (Chair)
Mark Robinson
William Russell
Deborah Shaw Marquardt (Vice Chair)
Nick Wheeler
Daniel Winterfeldt

PROGRAMME SUPPORTERS

PUBLIC FUNDING
Arts Council England, London
British Council
European Commission Representation in the UK

CHARITABLE DONATIONS
American Friends of the Royal Court
Martin Bowley Charitable Trust
The Brim Foundation*
Gerald Chapman Fund
City Bridge Trust
Cowley Charitable Trust
The H and G de Freitas Charitable Trust
The Edmond de Rothschild Foundation*
Do Well Foundation Ltd*
The Dorset Foundation
The John Ellerman Foundation
The Epstein Parton Foundation*
The Eranda Foundation
Genesis Foundation
J Paul Getty Jnr Charitable Trust
The Golden Bottle Trust
The Goldsmiths' Company
The Haberdashers' Company
Paul Hamlyn Foundation
Jerwood Charitable Foundation
Marina Kleinwort Charitable Trust
The Leathersellers' Company
Frederick Loewe Foundation*
John Lyon's Charity
The Andrew W Mellon Foundation
The Laura Pels* Foundation*
Jerome Robbins Foundation*
Rose Foundation
Royal Victoria Hall Foundation
The Peter Jay Sharp Foundation*
The Steel Charitable Trust
John Thaw Foundation
The Garfield Weston Foundation

CORPORATE SUPPORTERS & SPONSORS
BBC
Bloomberg
Coutts & Co
Ecosse Films
French Wines
Grey London
Kudos Film & Television

MAC
Moët & Chandon
Oakley Capital Limited
Sky Arts
Smythson of Bond Street

BUSINESS ASSOCIATES, MEMBERS & BENEFACTORS
Auerbach & Steele Opticians
Bank of America Merrill Lynch
Hugo Boss
Lazard
Louis Vuitton
Oberon Books
Savills
Vanity Fair

INDIVIDUAL MEMBERS

ICE-BREAKERS
Anonymous
Rosemary Alexander
Lisa & Andrew Barnett
Mrs Renate Blackwood
Ossi & Paul Burger
Mrs Helena Butler
Mr Claes Hesselgren & Mrs Jane Collins
Mark & Tobey Dichter
Ms P Dolphin
Elizabeth & James Downing
Virginia Finegold
Louisa Lane Fox
Charlotte & Nick Fraser
Alistair & Lynwen Gibbons
Mark & Rebecca Goldbart
Mr & Mrs Green
Sebastian & Rachel Grigg
Mrs Hattrell
Steven & Candice Hurwitz
Mrs R Jay
David Lanch
Yasmine Lever
Colette & Peter Levy
Watcyn Lewis
Mr & Mrs Peter Lord
David Marks QC
Nicola McFarland
Jonathan & Edward Mills
Ann Norman-Butler
Emma O'Donoghue
Georgia Oetker
Michael & Janet Orr
Mr & Mrs William Poeton
Really Useful Theatres
Mr & Mrs Tim Reid
Mrs Lois Sieff OBE
Nick & Louise Steidl
Torsten Thiele
Laura & Stephen Zimmerman

GROUND-BREAKERS
Anonymous
Moira Andreae
Nick Archdale
Charlotte Asprey
Jane Attias*
Caroline Baker
Brian Balfour-Oatts

Elizabeth & Adam Bandeen
Ray Barrell
Dr Kate Best
Dianne & Michael Bienes
Mr & Mrs Philip Blackwell
Stan & Val Bond
Neil & Sarah Brener
Miss Deborah Brett
Sindy & Jonathan Caplan
Gavin & Lesley Casey
Sarah & Philippe Chappatte
Tim & Caroline Clark
Carole & Neville Conrad
Kay Ellen Consolver & John Storkerson
Clyde Cooper
Ian & Caroline Cormack
Mr & Mrs Cross
Andrew & Amanda Cryer
Alison Davies
Noel De Keyzer
Polly Devlin OBE
Rob & Cherry Dickins
Denise & Randolph Dumas
Robyn Durie
Glenn & Phyllida Earle
Allie Esiri
Margaret Exley CBE
Celeste & Peter Fenichel
Margy Fenwick
Tim Fosberry
The Edwin Fox Foundation
John Garfield
Beverley Gee
Mr & Mrs Georgiades
Nick & Julie Gould
Lord & Lady Grabiner
Richard & Marcia Grand*
Nick Gray
Reade & Elizabeth Griffith
Don & Sue Guiney
Jill Hackel & Andrzej Zarzycki
Mary & Douglas Hampson
Sally Hampton
Sam & Caroline Haubold
Anoushka Healy
Mr & Mrs Johnny Hewett
Gordon Holmes
The David Hyman Charitable Trust
Mrs Madeleine Inkin
Nicholas Jones
Nicholas Josefowitz
Dr Evi Kaplanis
David P Kaskel & Christopher A Teano
Vincent & Amanda Keaveny
Peter & Maria Kellner*
Philip & Joan Kingsley
Mr & Mrs Pawel Kisielewski
Maria Lam
Larry & Peggy Levy
Daisy & Richard Littler
James & Beatrice Lupton
Kathryn Ludlow
David & Elizabeth Miles
Barbara Minto

Ann & Gavin Neath CBE
Murray North
Clive & Annie Norton
William Plapinger & Cassie Murray*
Andrea & Hilary Ponti
Wendy & Philip Press
Julie Ritter
Mark & Tricia Robinson
Paul & Gill Robinson
William & Hilary Russell
Julie & Bill Ryan
Sally & Anthony Salz
Bhags Sharma
Mrs Doris Sherwood
The Michael and Melanie Sherwood Charitable Foundation
Tom Siebens & Mimi Parsons
Richard Simpson
Anthony Simpson & Susan Boster
Samantha & Darren Smith
Brian Smith
Sandi Ulrich
The Ury Trust
Amanda Vail
Matthew & Sian Westerman
Mr & Mrs Nick Wheeler
Carol Woolton
Katherine & Michael Yates*

BOUNDARY-BREAKERS
Katie Bradford
Lydia & Manfred Gorvy
Ms Alex Joffe
Steve Kingshott
Emma Marsh
Paul & Jill Ruddock

MOVER-SHAKERS
Anonymous
Mr & Mrs Ayton
Cas Donald
Lloyd & Sarah Dorfman
Duncan Matthews QC
Ian & Carol Sellars
Edgar and Judith Wallner

HISTORY-MAKERS
Eric Abraham & Sigrid Rausing
Miles Morland

MAJOR DONORS
Rob & Siri Cope
Daniel & Joanna Friel
Jack & Linda Keenan*
Deborah & Stephen Marquardt
The David & Elaine Potter Foundation
Lady Sainsbury of Turville
NoraLee & Jon Sedmak*
Jan & Michael Topham
The Williams Charitable Trust

*Supporters of the American Friends of the Royal Court (AFRCT)

Wastwater

Characters

Harry
Frieda

Lisa
Mark

Sian
Jonathan
Alain
Dalisay

One

June 25th, 9 p.m.

A greenhouse on land adjacent to a large garden of a converted farmhouse outside Sipson in Middlesex. Evening.

Harry *is twenty-two.*

He looks all about him for a while. It's raining heavily. He watches it.

It stops. He sings the opening of 'Habanera' from Bizet's Carmen *to himself.*

Frieda *enters. She is sixty.*

Frieda   Harry? Harry love?

Harry   Hi.

Frieda   What are you doing out here sweetheart?

Harry   I'm sorry. I was just having a look at the view.

Frieda   I've been looking for you for ages. Have you been out here all this time?

Harry   Yeah. I'm sorry. I didn't realise you were looking for me.

Frieda   That's okay. I did call.

Harry   I didn't hear you. I must have been miles away.

Frieda   Well, that wouldn't be entirely out of character would it, love?

Harry *smiles at her.*

Frieda   It's nine o'clock.

Harry   Right.

Frieda   If your plane's at twenty past twelve you need be at the airport at half past ten.

Harry   I know.

Frieda   What time's the bus?

Harry   There's one just before ten. That'll give me loads of time.

Frieda   I wish you'd let me give you a lift. I don't want you to be late.

Harry   I won't be.

Frieda   You know what they can be like.

Harry   I'll be fine. Stop worrying.

Frieda   I know. Sorry.

The rain's stopped.

Harry   Yes.

Frieda   Everything's soaked.

It's still light considering what time it is.

You didn't get wet?

Harry   No, I sheltered under the branches. The branches were surprisingly resistant to the rain. I watched it like I was watching something on television. I climbed over the fence and came in here when it got really heavy.

Frieda   Are you not cold?

Harry   No.

Frieda   Would you like me to get you a jumper?

Harry   No thank you. I'm honestly fine. I wish you'd stop worrying about me. Did you get some sleep?

Frieda   A bit.

Harry   Did you?

Frieda   No.

Harry   Have you eaten some supper? I left you some chilli.

Frieda   I saw, thank you. I'll eat after you've gone.

Harry   You won't. You should eat something, Frieda. You're being silly. You've got yourself wound up.

She looks at him.

Frieda   Here's one.

An aeroplane flies overhead. It is tremendously loud. It's odd against the beauty of the garden. They wait for it to pass.

Harry   It's a completely clear sky now.

Frieda   Yes, it is rather, isn't it?

Harry   No turbulence at all.

Frieda   It's a bit boring really.

Harry   You should have seen them earlier.

Frieda   I watched some of them from the kitchen.

Harry   One of them must have dropped about two hundred feet.

Frieda   I love it when that happens.

What? What are you smiling about?

Harry   I'm thinking about Sheila. Is she very relieved about the runway repeal?

Frieda   She's beside herself.

Harry   I bet you're slightly disappointed. I bet you probably wanted to move now, didn't you?

Frieda   No. A bit I did.

Harry   I quite liked it. The idea of razing a whole town.

Frieda   Yes. I did too rather.

Harry   It's a matter of economics not ideology, you know?

Frieda   I told Sheila that.

Harry   As soon as they find the money they'll start planning again. You can move then.

She smiles at him.

Frieda   Are you all packed?

Harry   Course I am.

Frieda   I've got your address. When I find all the things you've forgotten I'll send them on to you.

Harry   Thanks.

Frieda   Have you got your passport?

Harry   In my bag.

Frieda   And your phone?

He turns to look at her. Slightly exasperated.

Have you got your debit card?

He laughs a bit.

Don't laugh.

He receives a text on his phone. Takes it out. Looks at it. Texts something quickly. Puts it away.

Harry   Well, you're being a bit bonkers.

Frieda   I'm not. I'm just being a mother.

Harry   Yeah.

Frieda   It's a habit I've learned to acquire.

He looks at her. Smiles.

Harry   The moon's out.

She feels the back of her calf.

Frieda   Oh look.

Harry   What?

Frieda   I'm bleeding a bit.

Harry   Are you?

Frieda   I cut my leg.

Harry How did you do that?

Frieda Climbing over the fence to get in here.

Harry Come here.

He bends down. He touches her cut. He has a packet of tissues in his back pocket. He takes one out and wipes her calf. She winces.

Frieda What are you doing?

Harry Does that hurt?

Frieda Course it doesn't hurt. It's just a graze.

Harry I can't believe you didn't notice it. What are you like?

Frieda I know. I'm sorry.

Harry Clean that properly after I've gone. Get a plaster on it. It'll get infected.

Frieda Don't be hysterical. Honestly. Talk about a bewildering over-reaction!

The thing you don't know about me, Harry, is I'm a bit of a savage.

Harry That's not true.

Frieda It is, you know.

Harry No. You're soft as shit.

Frieda You have to be a bit of a savage to survive you lot.

He looks at her. Looks away again.

Harry I might change my name when I get there.

Frieda Don't be stupid. Harry's a lovely name.

Harry Yeah, but I bet I could think of a better one. Horatio. Bartholomew. Isimbard. What? Isimbard's a great name.

Frieda Norman.

Harry   *Norman?*

Frieda   That was my dad's name.

Harry   I don't think I'm going to choose Norman, Frieda. That'd be ridiculous.

Frieda   Yeah.

Some time.

Harry   What was he like? Your dad?

Frieda   What was he like?

Harry   Were you more like him or were you more like your mum?

Frieda   I've no idea. I think that's for other people to say.

Harry   I wish I'd met her, your mum.

Frieda   She was quite a strange lady.

Harry   Like you then.

Frieda   And we never saw him at all. He worked abroad a lot of the time, which was unusual in those days. I remember his hair mainly. He had hair that was terribly stubbly. It was uneven and a horrible brown colour. He had eyes as hard as wood. After he died my mum confessed that she loved him far more than she loved us.

He looks at her. He receives a text on his phone. Takes it out. Looks at it. Texts something quickly. Puts it away.

Harry   Can I ask you something?

Frieda   Go on.

Harry   Have you heard from Sian?

Frieda   No.

Harry   Are you in touch with her?

Frieda   No, love, I'm not.

Harry   You better not be, Frieda.

Frieda   I'm not, love.

Harry   You better not be lying. I can always tell when people are lying.

Frieda   Don't, please.

Harry   The way she treated you. The things she did to you.

Frieda   She was just scared.

Harry   Is that what people do when they're scared? Is that how people behave?

Frieda   Sometimes it is, love, yes.

She used to hate it here. She hated the darkness. And the quiet. And how green everything was. I think she was very unhappy while she was here, I'm afraid. But out of the lot of you she was the only one who was. You weren't, were you, Harry?

Harry   I'm not even going to answer that.

Another plane flies overhead. They watch it again.

Frieda   Where are your socks, Harry?

Harry   I forgot to put some on.

Frieda   What do you mean? How could you forget to put your socks on for goodness' sake? I told you. I left some out for you. I washed them.

Harry   I packed all those. I'm sorry.

Frieda   I don't want an apology, I want you to stop doing it.

He receives a text on his phone. Takes it out. Looks at it. Texts something quickly. Puts it away.

Harry   Well, that's one thing you won't have to worry about from now on isn't it?

Frieda   Have you spoken to Laura?

Harry   This morning.

Frieda   How is she?

Harry   She's a bit upset. She kept crying. It was really annoying.

Frieda   Is she going to go over and see you?

Harry   No. I told her not to. I don't even like her all that much.

Frieda   Harry.

He receives a text on his phone. Takes it out. Looks at it. Texts something quickly.

Put it away.

Harry   Sorry.

He puts his phone away.

Frieda   For God's sake, it's like a kind of tic.

Harry   Yeah.

Frieda   I wish I could find out what you wrote half the time.

Harry   Well, you can't. Nosey.

Frieda   I'm going to steal it when you're not looking. I'll take advantage of you being distracted by your last-minute packing and nick your phone and go through your sent messages after you've gone.

Harry   You would as well.

Frieda   I know. And then I'll investigate your internet history.

Harry   I delete it.

Frieda   Do you honestly think that would stop me? Don't you know anything about computers?

Will there be a computer at the centre?

Harry   I'd have thought so, Frieda.

Frieda Will you have access to it?

I'll send you an email.

Harry You better had.

Frieda I was looking on the map. Across the strait from the Island, just south-east of Vancouver city, there's a place called Surrey. That made me laugh for ages. You're flying thousands of miles to move to Surrey. You could just go round the M25.

I might leave, you know.

Harry Where would you go?

Frieda Somewhere mountainous. With proper mountains, not just hills. Mountains with snow on.

Harry Don't be daft. You wouldn't ever do that.

Frieda Or I might come with you.

Harry Might you?

Frieda I could trace orcas. I could keep a record of whale sightings. I could do that easily.

Don't go.

I can't believe I said that out loud. Ignore me, I'm being silly. I don't mean it. I do really. Normally with you lot I'm secretly glad to see the back of you. With you it's completely different.

Harry Can I confess something to you, Frieda?

I feel guilty about Gavin.

Frieda Do you?

Harry All the time. The past year especially so.

Frieda That's not necessarily a bad thing, love.

Harry It feels bad. It feels dreadful if the truth be told.

Frieda It was an accident.

Harry Yeah. It wasn't really though.

Frieda   You had an accident.

Harry   I should have stopped him from getting in the car, Frieda.

Frieda   Yes, you should have done, but you didn't.

Harry   Everything round this whole area is making me feel ashamed.

I wrote a big long letter to his mum last night. It took me hours and hours. It said, 'Dear Gavin's stupid Mum. You are a stupid fat cow and I fucking hate you and if Gavin was alive today he'd say exactly the same thing, you miserable cow. But he isn't.' It went on and on in that vein for ages.

Frieda   What did you do with it?

Harry   I posted it. Nobody writes letters any more, do they? There's no way on earth I could possibly stay. I'd feel sick.

Frieda   You wouldn't.

Harry   I'd go insane.

Frieda   Don't be silly.

You could go next year. It's not like they're going to close the centre. They'd keep your job for you. Just write to them. Ask them.

He looks at her.

Some time.

Harry   I like elm trees.

Frieda   They're rare round here now.

Harry   A hundred years ago there were twenty million elm trees in England. Now it's in the hundreds.

Frieda   There used to be an avenue of them running behind the farm.

Harry   We are living in the middle of an ice age, did you know that?

Frieda   I have to confess I didn't Harry, no.

Harry   For most of its physical history our planet has been uninhabitably hot.

Frieda   I see.

Harry   There are brief times that last normally ten or twenty million years when it can become uninhabitably cold. This last happened about one and a half million years ago. This was the start of the most recent ice age. The Pleistocene Period.

Frieda   The Plastocene Period?

Harry   Shut up, Frieda, this is important. Twelve thousand years ago the ice began to thaw. It was the start of what is known as an interglacial. When the ice thawed life flourished. These warm periods happen every now and then. The ice thaws but it doesn't melt away completely, does it? There's ice now, isn't there? There are a hundred thousand glaciers in the world. There are glaciers in New Zealand, aren't there? And Asia. And South America. These warm periods normally last between ten and fifteen thousand years. We've maybe a millennium or two of thawing left. Probably much less. The freezing can start very suddenly. We're living through an infinitesimal moment in the history of the planet. It will end. I rather like the pathos of that.

It's all Charlie Cooper's fault.

Frieda   Is it?

Harry   Well, not just his fault. Farmers in general. All farmers. Ever.

Frieda   Right. Not just organic lamb farmers.

Harry   We should never have started farming.

Frieda   No.

Harry   Homo sapiens is a hunter-gatherer. It's how they're built anatomically. You start farming, you start producing more food for more people. So that rather than breeding according to your food supply you start raising the food supply to feed the population. It changes everything for the worse. You start draining your natural resources. You divert the water supply. You pollute the atmosphere. You develop social hierarchies that had never existed before. You start to feed the section of the population that has the highest economic or physical strength to the point where they actually over-feed and became obese. And you let another section of the population starve. This never happens when you hunt bison and gather berries. None of the catastrophes of human history would have happened if we'd not decided to farm.

Frieda Or any of the good things, Harry.

Harry I hope they flipping do build the runway. We want a runway. We need to move.

Frieda You do.

Harry We all do.

Frieda Yeah, but you do especially.

Harry It's like we've become nomadic again.

Frieda It's like you have.

Harry Oh, everybody gets very upset about it and agitated and they make all kinds of calls to radio phone-ins and sign all manner of electronic petitions. But you try telling somebody nowadays that they're going to live in the same place all their life and never leave it or go on holiday or anything like that and they'd look at you with a look of just horror. That would be their idea of hell. Thousands and thousands of years ago we made a terrible, terrible mistake. And it's sat under everything we've done since. And it will sit under everything we ever do. And we can't change it.

Frieda I love this.

Harry What?

Frieda Sitting here watching you talking.

Harry Frieda, are you even listening to what I'm saying?

Frieda   Of course I am.

Harry   You're not, are you?

Frieda   I am, you know.

Harry   I can't possibly stay here – you know that, don't you?

Frieda   Yes. No. I've no idea.

Harry   It's absolutely nothing to do with you so don't get self-pitying on me.

Frieda   I'm not. I wasn't. I'm the least self-pitying person in the world.

Harry   Do you like that barn?

Frieda   Do I like what?

Harry   That barn, do you like it?

Frieda   It's a barn, Harry.

Harry   I set fire to it once. I came into that field once and I set fire to the barn. Don't worry. It was before I came to your house. Years before. You probably heard about it, didn't you? They must have put it in my file.

Frieda   I don't remember.

Harry   I bet you do, and you're lying to be nice. I can't believe they let me come somewhere so close to it. I wonder if they did it on purpose.

There was a time when I was about twelve that I had the feeling that the newspapers were all going a bit backwards. It was like the headlines on the newspapers I was reading were actually about things that were going to happen the next day. I thought I read this headline that said that I burnt to death in a fire so I thought, to be honest to the news, because I didn't think it was right to lie about the news, that the best thing I could do was actually set fire to something. Watch it burn for a little bit. And burn inside it. The police came. Firemen came and put it out. I got in a lot of trouble.

I wonder what I'd do if the same thing happens when I get to Canada. I think I've decided I'm better off not believing everything I read in the papers.

It's getting late. I should get going.

Frieda   Will you do me a favour?

Harry   Go on.

Frieda   It's a bit silly. Will you go back to the house and turn the lights in the living room out and come back out here and stay with me for a bit before you leave. Just for a bit.

Harry   It's twenty past nine. The bus is leaving in half an hour.

He goes.

She waits on her own.

The lights from the house are turned off. The stage darkens.

Harry *comes back.*

Some time.

Harry   It's beautiful.

They count the stars for a bit.

I hope Sian never comes back again.

Frieda   She won't.

Can I tell you something, Harry?

Harry   Of course you can.

Frieda   You smell of wee a bit.

Harry   I know. It's awful isn't it? Four of my trousers do now. It's 'cause I drink so much coffee. I have a constantly full bladder and sometimes it does leak a bit.

Frieda   Well, for crying out loud, you should go to a doctor.

Harry   I know.

Frieda   I can't believe I didn't make you go to a doctor. Why don't you go to a doctor?

Harry   I'm terrified of doctors.

Frieda   Silly. Are you crying?

He doesn't appear to be crying in any way.

Harry   A little I am, yes.

I'm absolutely going in ten minutes flat.

Frieda   When you lot leave you all say that you'll come back and visit and none of you ever have apart from Sian.

So don't say you will because you won't.

You should know it doesn't make me angry, so don't think that. It's just something that happens when you foster.

I never get angry with you lot.

Harry   You bloody do.

Frieda   Not really, I don't. I get cross. Not angry. I never get angry with you because I never recognise myself in you. That's what makes parents angry. The things they recognise of themselves in their children. They love the characteristics their children share with their spouses.

Harry   Not all of them.

Frieda   Yes. And they hate the characteristics they share with themselves. I never have that.

Harry   You've got cross with me loads of times.

What's made you the crossest, do you think?

Frieda   Your tantrums. You couldn't half throw a tantrum when you wanted to.

Harry   I still can.

Frieda   And when you first came and I'd drive you to school and you'd refuse to leave me and you'd hold on to the car door and not let go.

I thought I must be doing something right. I hated it. I just wanted you to let go.

I won't ask you to change your mind again, but don't think I don't want you to because I do with every bit of me.

I bought you this.

She brings out an envelope from her cardigan and gives it to him.

There's a thousand pounds' worth of Canadian dollars in there. You'll be doing me a favour if the first thing you do is open a bank account and put the money in there and I hope I can trust you to do that.

Harry   You can.

Frieda   I hope so.

Harry   Thank you.

Frieda   That's the last, Harry. It's not a bottomless pit, love.

Harry   I know.

Frieda   That's all I've got.

Don't die. Will you?

Harry   No, all right.

Frieda   I mean never. Don't ever die.

Harry   Okay.

Frieda   Or do any crimes or take far too many drugs or drink yourself stupid or things like that. You have the potential to achieve anything you want. Don't waste that. And there'll be times in the future when you'll think of me and you'll think, probably, what an old cunt. Everybody thinks that about their parents eventually. Normally when they get to be about twenty-eight. But try to remember too that I do love you and I did love you and I will carry on loving you. And I hope one day you'll forgive me for everything I did wrong which I know was a lot but I did try my best. Honestly.

Harry   Shut up.

Frieda   Yeah.

Harry   You're being really strange.

Frieda   I know.

Harry   I'm a bit shocked, I have to admit. I'd never use the 'c' word around you.

Another plane passes. They watch it.

Frieda   And never hate yourself.

Harry   What?

Frieda   There are things which *you'll* have done or which *you'll* do which will live with you for ever and ever. You can't change it. You'll wish you could. You'll try. You won't be able to.

Harry   I'm going now.

Frieda   Yes.

Harry   I don't want to be late. Do me a favour and stay out here. Don't come in the house with me. Say goodbye here and I'll pull the front door after me. I'll even keep my keys because I know that will make you feel better.

Frieda   Look. Are you sure you don't want a lift?

Right. I won't press it.

Harry   I'll ring you when I get through the check-in.

Frieda   Yes.

Harry   And I'll ring you tomorrow as well. I'll figure out a good time with the time difference and everything.

Frieda   Don't worry about that. Just ring me when you land.

Harry   Could I have a hug?

Frieda   Of course you can. You're so silly. Come here.

He takes one step towards her. She opens her arms. Sudden black.

Two

June 23rd, 9 p.m.

A room at the Crowne Plaza Hotel, Heathrow Airport.

It's a modern, rather beautiful room.

It has a large bed.

There is a large, plasma-screen television. A large screen for a computer. A digital radio.

A large window behind beautiful curtains.

It's raining heavily outside. The rain stops.

Mark *is thirty.* **Lisa** *is forty-two.*

Mark   What's he like?

Lisa   I never know how to answer that.

Mark   Why not?

Lisa   I was thirty-two when I met him. I've only known him for ten years. But in those ten years it's like I've spent every waking moment when I've not been at work with him. It's like he's kind of part of my metabolism or something. It's like asking me what my hair's like.

Mark   Are you nervous?

Lisa   I'm a bit terrified.

Mark   Don't be.

Lisa   It's not really something you can avoid, is it?

Mark   Your palms are sweaty.

Lisa   I know. I'm sorry.

Mark   Do you want to go and have a wash or something?

Lisa   Well. Maybe. Maybe. Maybe. Not really. No. How was work?

Mark   I was a bit distracted.

Lisa   By what?

Mark   By coming here. By you.

Lisa   That's nice. How were the students?

Mark   I don't really want to talk about my work.

Lisa   No. Please.

Beat.

Mark   The same as they always are. Indolent. Stroppy. Rich.

Lisa   Are any of them any good?

Mark   I don't know yet. It's too soon to tell.

Lisa   What do you mean?

Mark   Some of them can, you know. They can draw. They like drawing. They can paint. They can make stuff. I don't know if they can reimagine a world. I think they find it hard to give of themselves. And if they can, at their age, well, to be honest that's rather scary. They're too young. They're better off drawing accurate pictures of pieces of fruit and cans and the like. Calm down.

Lisa   I am calm.

Mark   You don't look it.

Lisa   I am. Have you seen the size of the shower head? In the bathroom?

Mark   Yeah.

Lisa   I've never seen a shower head like it.

Mark   You sound a bit scared of it.

Lisa   Not scared. Just taken aback.

Mark   We could have a shower.

Lisa   Yeah.

Mark   Should we?

Lisa   Yeah.

Mark   Now?

Lisa   In a bit.

Mark   You can see the airport.

Lisa   Yeah.

Mark   It's rather beautiful I think. People don't normally think that about airports. I do.

It's stopped raining. It's still light.

I like hotels.

Lisa   Do you? They always make me feel a bit . . .

Mark   What?

Lisa   This one's lovely.

Mark   Who do you think stays here normally?

Lisa   I've no idea.

Mark   Who would want to stay at such a beautiful hotel so close to an airport? Do people come here on business, do you think? Is it for incredibly posh people who have to change flights on their way to Australia or something like that?

Lisa   I don't know.

Mark   I like the way that the television welcomes you to your room. Every time I come into these rooms it catches me by surprise. I always wonder what would happen if they got my name wrong. There'd be a moment when you'd wonder if you'd walked into the wrong room.

Lisa   Or you'd think you'd turned into a different person.

Mark   You can watch television from the shower. They arrange it so the inside of the room means that wherever you stand you can see the television. Probably, the people who come here feel so lonely that they need the television to remind them that there's a world outside and that things are happening and they're not, you know, alone.

Lisa   And they always have the news on. If you watch it for too long they repeat the same stories, but every time they repeat a story they present it like it's the first time you're seeing it and you start to feel like you're going a bit mad.

A beat. He looks at her.

Mark   What does he do?

Your husband?

Lisa   He's a social worker.

Mark   Is that how you met him?

Lisa   No. We met at a group. I thought I told you this.

Mark   No.

Lisa   He was my sponsor. One day he told me he wanted to stop being my sponsor because he thought he was falling in love with me. Which is about as unprofessional as you can get. It's actually quite a serious violation of the code of conduct, but those things are fucking ridiculous anyway so we just kind of went for it. He has the most beautiful fingers. They're graceful.

Mark   What would he say if he knew you were here?

Lisa   I don't think he'd say a great deal. He tends to go quiet.

Mark   Shhh.

Lisa   What?

Mark   Can you hear that?

Lisa   What?

Mark   Next door.

Lisa   What about next door?

Mark   You can hear the people talking.

Lisa   What are they saying?

Mark   I don't know.

Lisa   What language are they speaking?

Mark   French, I think. It sounds French.

Lisa   Do you like my dress?

Mark   I think it's stunning.

Lisa   I wore it for you.

That's nice.

Mark   What is?

Lisa   Your smile.

Mark   Do you have any idea how sexy I think you are?

Lisa   How sexy?

Mark   Fucking very.

Lisa   Do you know what the sexiest thing somebody can do to another person is? No. Don't answer that. I'll tell you. It's hold their gaze. It's keep eye-contact. To do that. To not flinch. To not look away. How long do you think you could hold eye contact with me for?

Mark   Hours.

Lisa   I bet you couldn't.

Mark   I bet I could.

A plane lands near to their window. It is audible, even in the soundproofed room. It stops them.

Lisa   A plane.

Mark   Yeah.

Lisa   What's she called?

Mark   Who?

Lisa   Who do you think?

Mark   Clare.

Lisa   Where did you meet her?

Mark   At school. I've known her since we were four.

Lisa   Ha.

Mark   What?

Lisa   It's surprising to meet somebody who's known their partner for such a long time.

Mark   We didn't start going out when we were four.

Lisa   No.

Mark   That would be a bit odd.

We arrived on exactly the same day. We kind of gravitated to one another. I presumed that she knew her way around and so I followed her wherever she went. It was only years later that I learned that she thought the same thing of me.

Do you want something to drink?

Lisa   Maybe. That might be nice. We should get some champagne.

Mark   Champagne?

Lisa   I like champagne.

Mark   Let me look.

He goes to the minibar. He takes out a half bottle of champagne.

Hey. Look. Here we are.

He opens it and pours two glasses into the glasses that are sitting on a tray above the minibar. He gives her one. They drink.

Lisa   This is lovely. Thank you.

Mark   In Russia, I read once, when a doctor dies, they open a bottle of champagne on his death bed. I rather like that idea.

Lisa   You're not dying, are you?

Mark   No. Don't be stupid.

Lisa   Because that would make all this even weirder than it is already.

Mark   Do you think this is weird?

Lisa   I do, yeah.

Mark   Do you want to . . . ?

Lisa   Not yet.

Mark   Because I do, I think.

Lisa   I know. I could tell that. We've got hours. Silly.

He looks at her. Smiles.

He moves a small distance away from her.

Mark   I had some news at work today.

Lisa   News?

Mark   Six months ago I applied to go on a Fulbright exchange.

Lisa   What's that?

Mark   It's an exchange, the British Council pay for it. You swap colleges with a teacher in America. I found out today that I've been accepted on it. I'm going to the Minneapolis College of Art and Design.

Lisa   Gosh. When?

Mark   In September.

Lisa   How long for?

Mark   For a year.

Lisa   With Clare?

Mark   No. She's staying here. She has to work.

I'm a bit bewildered by it all. To be honest I completely forgot that I made the application. The Head of the College called me in to tell me. It took me about five minutes before I realised what he was going on about. I thought he'd got the wrong teacher. It's been a slightly disorientating past ten days.

Lisa Yes.

She looks at him. She puts her glass down.

Come here.

He does.

Hold your hand out.

He does.

Mark What are you doing?

Lisa I'm reading your palm.

Mark Why?

Lisa I want to figure out your future.

Mark Do you believe in all that?

She looks at him.

Lisa If I tell you something, will you be cross with me?

Mark Cross?

Lisa Have you seen this?

She shows him an area in the underside of her arm.

Mark What's that from?

Very quietly she sings the 'Habanera' from Bizet's Carmen. *She sings it beautifully.*

She stops.

She looks at him.

Lisa The group I used to go to, the group where I met Andrew, wasn't for alcoholics. It was for people who were addicted to narcotics. When I was your age I used to take heroin. I smoked it for about two years and then for about six months I started injecting it. If you want to leave now I wouldn't mind.

Mark   Why would I want to leave?

Lisa   Some people find it disgusting.

Mark   I don't.

Lisa   They get frightened. You hear things, don't you?

Mark   What kind of things?

Lisa   I started smoking it to help me get to sleep. The thing about my job is that people smoke a lot and they drink a lot and they drink a lot of coffee and Coca-Cola and things like that and I did that to the point where I couldn't get to sleep at night. I mentioned this to a colleague and he asked me if I'd ever thought about smoking some heroin to help me get off. Looking back now I realise that he was quite an odd man.

Mark   He sounds it.

Lisa   It's quite easy to get where I work.

Mark   I can imagine.

Lisa   Have you ever taken it?

Mark   No.

Lisa   I really love it. It makes you feel so happy. It makes you feel very relaxed. I took quite a lot of it after a while. After a couple of months I stopped getting it from work. It was quite easy to make contact with a dealer who wasn't going to rip me off so I used to go to him instead. I won't tell you his name, if you don't mind. The problem is that your tolerance levels build up and you need to use more to try and get the feeling back that you had the first time you took it. You can spend quite a lot of money. It did start to become a small problem. One day the man I was buying my heroin from asked me how I made the money to pay for it. I told him, you know, I get some from my parents and I work. He asked me what I did. I told him I was a police officer.

Mark   Did you?

Lisa   Yes. I did.

Mark   Why did you tell him that?

Lisa   Well because I am.

Mark   You could have lied.

Lisa   Why?

Mark   Wasn't it a bit compromising?

Lisa   Who to?

Mark   To you. To him. How did he react?

Lisa   He was a bit scared at first but you know. I reassured him. I calmed him down. I work in child protection. It's not drugs. You know?

Mark   Right.

Another plane passes by the window. She pauses to look towards it. She looks back.

Lisa   He asked me if that was enough money and I said no. And he said, 'Well. There *is* a way, if you want, that I could help you make a bit more money.' I asked him how and he said, 'Well, I find you very attractive.' I was like, right, sonny Jim, where are we going with this one and he was like, 'Have you thought about doing any acting?' I said no, and he said, 'Well. I'd like to make a film with you, would you like that?' Well. I'm thinking, OK. I've never actually made a film before so that's quite exciting and I said, 'What kind of film is it?' And he looked at me. Like. He did a funny little cheeky grin and he said, 'It's a porno.' He asked me how I felt about that. I asked him what it would involve doing and he said, 'Well, what do you think?' And, you know me. You know what I'm like. So I decided to say OK. But I draw the line. There are some things I won't do. I said, 'I won't do anal and I won't do animals and I won't do children, is that OK?' And he said that yes, it was OK. And so we did, actually. You know? I really liked him and I still do. I still really like him. I don't see him any more but if I saw him I wouldn't have anything to say against him. I know that sounds a bit odd but I do think at heart he's a good person. He was always very clean and he was always very concerned that I didn't get, you know, properly hurt. We go to this hotel and it's a hotel near Stansted Airport. In Essex. And there's me and him and his friend Jason. And the thing about Jason is that they obviously cast him carefully because he is nice and he is handsome and I was sitting in this car on the way to the hotel thinking you know. I don't mind, frankly. I don't mind. With him. That's OK. So we're sat there. And his friend Michelle, who's lovely. She's a bit younger than I am. And a bit thick. But she's nice. And he says, 'So you have to pretend that you've come home and you've found Jason fucking Michelle and Michelle is your daughter and what happens is you really. You like it. Yes? And you decide to join in.' Which is fine, isn't it, because in real life Michelle isn't actually my daughter, is she? We're just, you know, pretending. And it's a bit stupid because we have to cram the idea that this hotel room is my home into the story and it doesn't completely work. But you know? I'd never had sex with a woman and that was. We got quite giggly. It did make me feel old. And Jason was very gentle and even though it got a bit blokey at times it was fine. It was clean. They paid me £500 every time I made a film. Which for me at the time was quite a lot of money. After a while you get a bit immune to it. You assimilate it, I think is the word. One time he took me out to Epping Forest and he tied my hands and my ankles together and he put me in the boot of the car and we drove out there and filmed another man, not Jason, this Asian man, who he called David, opening the boot and dragging me out and there were seven men and they did have a wank and I had to try and suck their cocks for them while they were wanking and as many of them as possibly could had to try and cum in my hair or just on me somewhere. That was the only film I made where I did a bit of crying and he quite liked that and I decided to stop after that.

Silence.

Are you OK?

He nods.

Has that come as a surprise to you?

Mark   It has a little.

Lisa   I thought you needed to know.

Have you got eczema?

Mark *nods.*

Lisa   Don't scratch it. You'll make it worse.

He nods.

It is online. If you want we could find it. Would you like me to find it for you?

Mark   No.

Lisa   We could do.

Mark   I don't want you to.

Lisa   It would be a bit of a giggle. It's had over 24,000 hits. Its average rating is 78 per cent.

Mark   What does that mean?

Lisa   Well, when you watch a film you have to say whether you like it or not and 78 per cent of the people who've watched the film have thought it was good. Which means 22 per cent haven't. You can read their comments.

Mark   What do they say?

Lisa   You know.

Mark   No. What do they say about you?

Lisa   I'd rather not talk about it, if you don't mind.

Do you feel disgusted?

Mark   No.

Lisa   Do you want to go home?

Mark   No.

Lisa   Maybe you should. It might be for the best.

Mark   No.

Lisa   I honestly wouldn't mind if you did.

Mark   I don't want to.

Lisa   I wouldn't be upset. Don't worry about my feelings.

Mark   I'm not.

Lisa   Do you promise me?

Mark   How long did you do it for?

Lisa   I honestly don't remember.

Mark   What did Andrew say?

Lisa   I've never told him.

Mark   Have you ever told anybody?

What would they say if they found out at work?

Lisa   They wouldn't say a great deal. They'd fire me. I'd go to prison for a short time.

Mark   To prison?

Lisa   For abusing my position as a police officer.

Mark   I'm a little bit –

Lisa   I know. I'm sorry. Would you like to sit down?

He does.

She sits next to him.

You don't need to say anything. We could just sit here for a bit.

She holds his hand. She plays with it for a bit. She smells it. She compares it in size and shape of finger to her own hands. Then just holds it.

Where does she think you are? Clare?

Mark   She thinks I'm at home. She's gone to stay with her mother for the weekend. I told her I had to work. Which is true actually. I do have to work.

Lisa   Where does her mother live?

Mark   Outside Lancaster.

Lisa   Near the Lake District.

Mark   That's right.

Lisa   We used to go camping on Wastwater, when I was a little girl. It's the deepest lake in the country. It's surrounded by screes and mountains which mean it's never completely out of the shadow. It's terribly still. My dad told me that the stillness was a bit of a lie. 'It looks still, Lisa, but you should see how many bodies are hidden under there.' When I get a mental picture of my dad it's always there. He's always wearing his shorts. Cooking eggs on one of those little gas stoves you can get.

What's your dad like?

He looks at her for a while before he answers. He's a bit disorientated.

Lisa   It's funny, isn't it?

Mark   What is?

Lisa   You make one decision. It stays with you. It's like the consequences of it get into your bones. Am I being a bit mad?

Mark   No.

Lisa   I just thought. If we're going to do this there are some things you should know. For the sake of honesty.

Mark *nods.*

Lisa   Do you know what I'd like?

Mark   No.

Lisa   I'd like to see your art.

Mark   Would you?

Lisa   No. Actually. Not really. What's it like?

Mark   I've only started working again in the past six months.
I stopped for about four years. Four and a half years ago the
best student I ever taught was killed in a car accident. He was
a boy called Gavin Berkshire. He was astonishing. He and a
friend got drunk and got into a car and he drove it into a wall.
He died. His friend didn't, which always struck me as a little
unfair. After that I found it difficult to work at all. Just recently
I've started again. My work's become quite figurative. I make
paintings of people. This is very strange.

Lisa   Yes. Have you painted me?

Mark   No.

Lisa   Would you?

Mark   I don't think so.

I'm not good enough. To make it as a professional artist. If the
truth be told. I never will be. That's quite a hard thing to get
your head round.

Some time.

Lisa   Do you think you'll have children with Clare?

Mark   Maybe. One day.

Lisa   You'd make a good father.

Mark   Did you never want children?

She shakes her head.

Pause.

Lisa   My sister's got two children. They're nine and seven
now. She won't let me see them.

Some time.

I've never had sex with Andrew. I think it's because it reminds
me of that time. I mean this was twelve years ago, but even
so. I like to sleep with him. We do a lot of cuddling. We hold
hands a lot. We snuggle. It's not that I don't like sex. I just
prefer not to associate it with him. Is that stupid?

Mark   No.

Lisa   Because I do. Like sex, I mean.

Mark   Me too.

Lisa   And I very much want to have sex with you.

Mark   Well, that's good.

Lisa   Are you sure you're still in the mood?

Mark   I think so, yes.

Lisa   Because I wouldn't blame you if you felt the moment had kind of passed.

Mark   I don't.

Lisa   That's good.

If I had sex with you I think I'd like to keep my dress on, how would that be?

Mark   That would be − I'd like that.

Lisa   I think I'd like to blindfold you, Mark, too. Could I do that?

He nods.

I might tie you to a chair and blindfold you and tie your hands up so that you're not allowed to touch me no matter how much you want to. And you can't see me.

He nods.

This is the kind of thing I've been thinking about today. Is that a bit shocking?

Mark   No, it's good. I like it.

Lisa   One of the other things I've been thinking about, one of the things I wanted to do tonight, was I wanted you to hit me. How would you feel about that?

Mark   To hit you?

Lisa *nods.*

Mark *looks at her. He tries to say something and can't.*

Lisa   Do you think you could? Some people can do it and some people find it too difficult.

Do you think you could do it or would it be a bit tricky?

Mark *looks at her. He says nothing.*

Lisa   Have I scared you a bit? It's all right. I do understand.

Mark *looks at her. He says nothing.*

Lisa   Don't be scared. I didn't mean to scare you. It's not about hating me or hurting me or anything like that Mark. Don't panic. It's the opposite of that.

If I wanted you to stop I'd tell you to stop. We could make up a word. When I've done this before I've used the word 'water'. If I said the word 'water' then that would mean that you'd have to stop. It's our safe word. I promise you that if I got scared or unhappy or uncomfortable then I'd say the word 'water' and then you'd just stop. Would you like to try it do you think?

Mark   No.

Lisa   We could film it on your phone. That might be a giggle. Would you like that?

Mark   No.

Lisa   You could upload it. Tomorrow. When you get home. When Clare's gone to bed.

Mark   Stop it. I'm not going to hurt you. I'm not going to hit you. For God's sake!

Lisa   How old are you?

Mark   I'm thirty. You know that.

Lisa   That's it then.

Mark   What? What's it?

Lisa   You'll have a moment when you're older when you'll get it.

Mark   What are you talking about?

Lisa   If you'd seen some of the things that I see when I do my work. Or met some of the people I meet. The things they've done! It's just the same with them and the decisions they've made living in their bones, by the way.

Mark   I don't know what you're talking about.

Lisa   No. I'm sorry. I'm being odd. Touch my face.

He goes to her. He touches her face.

Mark   It's soft.

She holds his hand on her face. She kisses his hand and the top of his wrist.

Lisa   Your hands smell nice.

Mark   Do they?

Lisa   They smell like copper. Like you've been playing with coins or something like that.

Please. Please. I so want you to. Please.

He studies her.

Mark   I've never hit anybody.

Lisa   Has anybody ever hit you?

Mark   Not properly.

Lisa   What does that mean, 'not properly'?

Mark   A teacher kind of slapped me one time. Does that count?

Lisa   I don't know. Maybe. Why did he slap you?

Mark   Well, it's a bit stupid. And it didn't hurt or anything like that. It was a bit embarrassing, if the truth be told. He went all red. It didn't even properly connect properly. It was in the corridor and everything. He did get sacked afterwards which felt a bit extreme at the time, even from my point of view.

Lisa   Why did he slap you?

Mark   He made a pass at Clare. One time he asked her if she'd like to come and have a drink with him. We were in fifth year so it's not that big a deal but he did say, you know, when you leave if you want to stay in touch then you should just give me a call or something. I got a bit pissed off with it. We had a row in the corridor. He kind of slapped me. A bit like how a kind of stereotype of a girl would slap you.

I shouldn't have said anything to him. It was stupid that he got sacked.

Since I was small I've always wanted to walk across a desert. A big one. Like the Sahara. Or the Gobi. Or the Patagonian. Without any water. Or food or anything. Just to know what it would feel like.

Lisa   Yeah.

He hits her across her face.

They stare at one another. He hits her again.

She gasps. Holds her breath.

They stare at one another.

He hits her again.

She puts her hand to her face.

Are you OK?

Mark   I think so. Are you?

Lisa   Yes.

Wait here.

She goes into the bathroom.

He waits.

While she's in the bathroom she starts the shower running.

After a while she comes back out again.

She goes to the window. She opens it. She turns back to him.

Lisa   Do you believe in good people and bad people?

Mark   Yes.

Lisa   Me too. Absolutely. What are you?

Mark   I'm a good person.

Lisa   You so are. You're one of the best people in the whole world. I am too.

Mark   I know. I was thinking that while you were in the bathroom.

Lisa   We should get married. We could do it illegally. I could become a bigamist.

Mark   We could.

Lisa   You could bring me to Minneapolis. We could visit Prince. We could go to the Mall of America.

Mark   To where?

Lisa   There's a shopping mall outside of Minneapolis called the Mall of America. It's the biggest shopping mall in the world. Japanese tourists fly in just to go there. They go straight from the airport and then go straight back home again. We could go there.

While she's talking she turns the television on. It's BBC News 24. She turns the sound down and reads the sub-titles. As she talks she undresses a little. Maybe takes off a cardigan or her shoes.

Mark   We could.

Lisa   Go shopping. Buy clothes for each other. It's half past nine. It should be getting dark by now. Have you seen the sky?

Mark   Yeah.

Lisa   Have you ever seen a sky that colour before?

Mark   I don't think so.

Lisa   Is the sky meant to be that colour?

Mark   I don't know.

Lisa   We're better off in here.

Mark   Yes.

Lisa   Better off inside.

In the future the whole of the world will be like this, you know?

Mark   Like what?

She goes to the computer and turns it on. She goes online.

Mark *watches her do this and takes his shoes and socks off.*

She finds a porn site. She plays a porn video. It's importantly clear that's it's not her in the film. Maybe the actors are black or German, for example.

Lisa   Everybody will stay inside in beautiful rooms. With musky smelling hand-wash and nice mineral waters. And soft towels.

Mark   Yeah.

She sits on the bed with her back to him.

Lisa   What?

I'm being serious. Zip please.

He unzips the back of her dress.

Thank you.

Never call me Lise. People at work call me Lise all the time. I hate it.

Mark   OK. I didn't. I wouldn't.

Lisa   Are you crying?

Mark   No.

Lisa   You can do, you know? It's all right.

Mark   I'm not crying. What gives you the idea that I'm crying? Why would I be crying?

Lisa   'Heaven knows we need never be ashamed of our tears, for they are rain upon the blinding dust of earth overlying our hard hearts.'

Mark   What?

Lisa   Nothing.

She puts the radio on. It plays very uplifting commercial pop music.

She turns and looks at him before she comes back to the bed. She moves towards the bed.

Sudden black.

Three

June 23rd. 9 p.m.

A deserted warehouse on the periphery of Heathrow Airport.

There is a desk with a clipboard and a pen on it, two chairs, a bucket.

Sian *is twenty-five.* **Jonathan** *is forty-three.*

It's raining heavily outside. The rain stops.

Sian Do you like my dress?

No response.

Do you know what flowers these are?

Jonathan They look like roses.

Sian They're gardenias.

Jonathan They're a nice colour, Sian.

Sian Do you think they go well with my eyes?

Jonathan I. Er. Yes. I think.

Sian Can I tell you? You're wrong.

Do you know why?

Jonathan No.

Sian My eyes are two different colours. I've got one blue eye and one green eye.

Jonathan I can't tell that from here.

Sian No.

Thank you for coming. It's only just nine o'clock. You're early.

You didn't get wet, did you?

Jonathan No.

Sian Has the rain stopped?

Jonathan   Just now.

Sian   I bet you got the fright of your life when Alain called you, didn't you?

What happened to your nose?

Jonathan   My nose?

Sian   It's broken. What happened to it?

A pause.

Jonathan   I fell.

Sian   Did you?

Jonathan   I was a teacher. One time I slipped and fell down some stairs in the school where I taught. The floor was wet. It was rather embarrassing, as a matter of fact.

Sian   I fucking bet it was.

Jonathan   How did you get my number?

Sian   How do you think?

Jonathan   I don't know. That's why I'm asking.

Sian   Alain knows Stephen Cochrane.

So.

The penny drops.

Do you need to sit down?

Jonathan   No, thank you. I'm fine.

Sian   You don't look fine. You look a bit pale. A bit, 'Oh my God what in the name of all things wonderful have I gone and fucking done this time' kind of a pale.

Yes?

I'm right, aren't I?

Jonathan   I'm a bit cold.

Sian   All of a sudden?

Jonathan   It's very cold in here.

Sian   Funnily enough I don't mind that. That's never bothered me.

Jonathan   There's no heating in here at all.

Sian   Why would there be?

Jonathan   And there's no natural light. I find it a bit oppressive.

I think I would like to sit down.

She smiles at him.

Sian   What did you teach?

Jonathan   I'm sorry?

Sian   When you were a teacher?

Jonathan   Maths.

Sian   In a private school or a comprehensive?

Jonathan   In a private school. A fee-paying boarding school. I stopped teaching after ten years. Well, I say that. I actually mean I stopped teaching in schools. I started teaching in teacher training college.

Sian   Can I tell you?

Jonathan   What?

Sian   I honestly don't give a shit.

Where's your money?

Jonathan   In my car.

Sian   Good lad. Are you sure it's safe out there?

Jonathan   Do you think it might not be?

Sian   Funny, isn't it?

Jonathan   What?

Sian   The things we do!

A plane lands nearby.

Jonathan   What was that?

Sian   What?

Jonathan   That noise.

Sian   It was a plane, Jonathan, what do you think it was? You're very jumpy, aren't you?

How's your wife?

Jonathan   Please don't.

Sian   Don't what?

Jonathan   Look. I'm here, aren't I? I've brought my money with me, haven't I? You don't need to –

I never made a deal with Stephen Cochrane.

Sian   He said.

Jonathan   We exchanged three emails.

Sian   I read them.

Jonathan   We spoke once over the phone.

Sian   From a room in a Holiday Inn in Derby, he said. Classy.

Jonathan   We met once.

Sian   Yes.

Jonathan   We changed our mind.

Sian   He found that a little, what's the word? A little fucking frustrating to say the least. I think would be the word he used.

Jonathan   I haven't done anything wrong.

She smiles.

Sian   Where do you think these puddles come from?

Jonathan   I've no idea.

Sian   What do you think they're made of?

Jonathan   Water. Maybe. Oil.

Sian   Do you think so?

Jonathan   I don't know.

Sian   Are you very scared?

You look it. Do you know what would happen to you if you got caught?

Jonathan   What are you talking about?

Sian   What's the worst thing you've ever done? Before today?

Jonathan   I've not done anything.

Sian   Don't you think?

There is some time. He thinks.

Jonathan   When I was a teacher I hit one of my pupils. Hard. Across the face.

Sian   Why?

Jonathan   He smirked at me.

Sian   Smirked?

Jonathan   He suggested I was having a relationship with one of the girls in the sixth form. He stuck a poster about it up on the library notice board.

Sian   Were you?

Jonathan   Of course I wasn't. What kind of a person do you think I am?

Sian   I have no fucking idea, Jonathan, you tell me.

A pause.

Do you know what the worst thing I ever did was?

Jonathan   I can't imagine.

Sian When I was twelve I drowned a dog. At the back of the house where my first foster parents lived. Just south-east of Stoke. They had a house with a huge field and a lake behind it. Well, I say a huge field. It was more like a very big unusually attractive recreational ground. And I say lake, it was more like, what? A pond? My first foster father had a brother called Clive who lived in Swansea. He was a fucking rat-hole. He used to come and visit us. He had this dog. I say dog. It was more of a bundle of shit than a dog. He used to threaten me with it. He fell asleep. I took the dog for a walk. Hit it over the back of its skull with a brick that my first foster father kept in the garage because one day he was hoping to build his own extension. Stunned it. It became comically weary. Wobbled about a bit. I dragged it by its lead to the pond. Dragged it in. Held its head under the water. It didn't react for a long time. And then it did. Its legs got all tense. It thrashed about.

I had a heck of a time explaining why my skirt was wet. I can tell you that for nothing.

How long have you been going grey for?

It didn't just happen when Alain rang, did it? Or did it? I bet it did, didn't it?

I like your watch. Where did you get that from?

Jonathan It was my father's.

Sian I so knew you were going to say that. Is anything you say ever not sickeningly predictable? Can I ask you? Please, for one fucking second, could you please keep your fingers still. Please.

Do you like my feet?

Are you one of those men who likes girls' feet?

We've found her.

Jonathan What?

Sian You so fucking heard me, Jonathan, don't try and pretend that you didn't. Fuck. Alain's with her now. He's been with her since Tuesday.

Jonathan   Can I leave, please?

Sian   What do *you* think?

It's odd, isn't it? You connect to an unsecured network in Charles de Gaulle airport even though you're given all the warning in the fucking world that the information you send may not be secured. You don't even think for a second what that actually might mean.

Later you go to a website which you know is perfectly safe. You check the hit rate. Two and a half million hits in the last twenty-four hours. It's mainstream. It's very straightforward. It gets more hits than the *Guardian* sports page, for fuckssake. You've checked! And a photograph leads you to another website. And on that website there is an advert that leads you to a third website. And the further you go the less, what, professional? Yes. Professional-seeming these other websites are, but you keep going. Because nobody knows. You're absolutely sure of it. Nobody knows. Nobody knows.

You know what, Jonathan?

Everybody knows.

She's older than you suggested to Stephen.

Jonathan   I want to go home, please.

Sian   She's nine.

A plane lands nearby.

It's surprisingly high. Isn't it?

Jonathan   What is?

Sian   The ceiling here.

Jonathan   My. My. My. My. My circumstances have changed since my conversations with Stephen.

Sian   'My. My. My. My. My – ' what the fuck are you going on about? What the fuck is the matter with your mouth?

Jonathan   My circumstances have changed since my last conversation with Stephen.

Sian   Are you saying you're no longer in the, what? No longer in the market. Is that what you're trying to imply?

Do you honestly think you have any choice in the matter?

This is the consequence of what you did.

Jonathan   I didn't do anything.

She smiles at him.

She picks up the clipboard and pen and starts reading from the papers on it.

Sian   I need to ask you some questions.

Jonathan   What?

Sian   They're kind of like a test.

Jonathan   A test?

Sian   A personality test.

Jonathan   I don't think I understand you.

Sian   I need to figure out your personality.

Jonathan   Why?

Sian   This is good.

Jonathan   What is?

Sian   Already you're giving me a big clue as to the nature of your personality. You're not really very trusting, for example.

Jonathan   Trusting?

Sian   Are you? You lack trust.

Jonathan   I feel sick.

Sian   There is a bucket.

Put your hand here.

She gets a pair of handcuffs from her pocket. She wraps her fist inside one of the handcuffs to wear it like a knuckle-duster.

She points to a very exact position on the table.

Jonathan   Why?

Sian   Always 'why' with you, isn't it? Why? Why? Why? Why? Is it meant to be a sign of intelligence? A sign of a spirit of inquiry? Is that what you think you're playing at, 'cause if it is I've got news for you, Jonnyboy, it's fucking unattractive.

Do you have the slightest idea how unpredictable we are?

He puts his hand exactly where she asked him.

Thank you.

Jonathan   I don't want to do this any more.

Sian   You see, I think you do.

How long did you try for? Seven years. How much money did you spend on the treatment? Fifty-one thousand eight hundred pounds. How many different agencies did you apply to? Eight. What was the principal cause for rejection? What was the principal cause of rejection? Jonathan, this is a serious fucking question and I expect an answer or I'll drive this handcuff through the top of your hand.

Do you think I won't?

Jonathan   We were rejected on grounds of health.

Sian   Why?

Jonathan   For a few years my wife was quite poorly. In 2005 she spent a few months in a hospital because of an illness that was a product of a kind of exhaustion.

Sian   She's from Cebu which is in the northern Philippines. She's tired because she's been travelling for two and a half weeks. She found the flying a little frightening. She doesn't speak much English. She's mixed race. She never knew her father but we suspect he was European.

Do you expect me to believe that you would have contacted Stephen in the first place, that you would have sent those emails or booked a room in a Holiday Inn in Derby in order to make that phone call or gone to meet him in a pub in Epping Forest if you didn't want to go through with it?

Change your circumstances back.

Jonathan   What do you mean?

Sian   Ring your wife. 'Guess what, sweetheart? I've got a surprise for you!'

Jonathan   Where is she?

Sian   Heathrow. Terminal 5. She'll be cleared by now. She'll have gone through arrivals. Or she'll be waiting to get through an interview at Passport Control. In one of those rooms with the two-way mirrors that people always stare through hoping to get a little sight of the men who wait behind there and spend all day watching them. She'll get through it very easily because she'll have been very prepared. She'll be here within the next half an hour. Or the next hour. Or the next three hours. Or the next four days. It depends.

Jonathan   On what?

Sian   What do you fucking think?

She puts the clipboard down again.

It's complicated being married sometimes, isn't it?

Jonathan   What?

Sian   I was married once.

I was married when I was eighteen. I married a man called Ian. He was fifteen years older than me. He was a painter. He painted landscapes. He was very, very good. He had an extraordinary eye for detail and for colour. He sold them in auctions. He was fucking loaded.

He was the son of a friend of my second foster mother. She's a woman called Frieda. She's from near here. She's from a small village called Sipson, just north of the motorway. She's absolutely beautiful. She looks about my age, which is annoying. I lived with her until I married Ian. She's lovely. Then when he went a bit – shall we say 'off'? – when he went a bit 'off', I went back and lived with her again.

There are reservoirs and parks near there that I used to wander around. They were going to destroy the whole village to make space to build the third runway. Can you imagine?

I divorced Ian when I was twenty-three. I consider it one of my many failures. My marriage. So I understand about how difficult it can be.

Keep your hand still.

If you didn't want to go through with it, why did you meet me?

He looks at her for a while before he answers.

Jonathan   On the phone, Alain sounded, he seemed to know an awful lot about me.

Sian   We do.

Jonathan   I got a bit nervous.

Sian   If you didn't want to go through with it, why did you withdraw all the money?

Jonathan   I was scared.

Sian   I don't believe you.

At 11.22 this morning you went to the Islington branch of the Co-Operative Bank on the corner of Upper Street and Pentonville Road and carried out a prearranged withdrawal of £31,000 in cash. You dealt with Charlotte Granger there. She's the Deputy Branch Manager. She doesn't work on the counters. If you want to speak to Charlotte Granger you need to make a fucking appointment. You rang your branch at 9.03 this morning and you made that appointment and you arranged the withdrawal and having made the withdrawal you went shopping. You went up Upper Street and bought a copy of the second Arctic Monkeys album, a decision which I find frankly bewildering, and you also bought a pair of fingerless gloves for your bicycle from the Halfords on Liverpool Road. You went to Pret A Manger and bought a hot meatball wrap and a bottle of still mineral water and having eaten them, on the tube probably or maybe on the walk from the shop to Angel tube station, you went into your office for five hours. You left at 6.00. You bought a bottle of shit New Zealand Semillon from the Oddbins on the way to Holborn tube and got out of Archway tube at 6.43. You spent about an hour at home. I haven't got a clue what you did there. Apart from checking your emails and watching fifteen minutes of news highlights on the BBC website. You must have left your house at eight o'clock in order to get here on time. My point being, Jonathan, that yours is not the behaviour of a man who's nervous. Is it? Well, is it? It's not, is it? No, of course it's not.

It's the behaviour of a man of clarity. It's clear-headed behaviour. It's decisive behaviour.

Have you wet your trousers?

I thought I could smell something.

Tell me you don't want to go through with it.

Tell me you don't want to go through with it.

Jonathan   What will happen if I –

Sian   Use your imagination.

Tell me you don't want to go through with it.

I'm going to count down from five to one and you've got until I get to one to tell me you don't want to go through with it.

Five. Four. Three. Two. One.

So.

I've got some questions for you. It's very important that you answer them quickly. It's very important you answer them honestly. The speed and clarity and honesty of your answers will have a bearing on what happens next. Do you understand?

Jonathan   I'm not sure.

Sian   It will help us decide if we're going to go through with the transaction or not.

Jonathan   What happens if my answers aren't right?

Suddenly she slams her fist, wrapped in the handcuffs, down on to the table by his hand.

He instinctively pulls it away.

Sian   Ooh. That was close. Put your hand back.

He does.

Thank you.

Stop crying. You're distracting me.

She picks up the clipboard and pen again. It takes her a beat or two to find the first question.

What's your favourite piece of music and why?

He looks at her for a moment.

Jonathan   Is that the first question?

Sorry, is that the first question?

Sian   Speed. Clarity. Honesty. Fuckball.

Bewildered, it takes him some time to think of an answer.

Jonathan   'Music for the End of Time' by Messiaen.

She writes something. She ticks two columns.

She waits for him to complete the second part of his answer.

I find its melody very beautiful although it is odd. I find the orchestration painful. It moves me that it was written entirely for the instruments that were available to him in the camp where he was imprisoned.

She writes something. She ticks two columns. Finds the next question.

Sian   Where's the furthest north you've ever travelled?

Jonathan   I went to Seattle once. I'm not sure if it's Seattle or Inverness. I spent a weekend in Inverness once. I don't know the exact er, latitude or – I think Seattle.

She writes something. She ticks two columns. Finds the next question.

Sian   Which part of air travel do you find most unsettling –
departure, flight or arrival?

Jonathan   Flight. I don't like turbulence. It didn't used to
bother me. Now I find it horrible. When the plane just drops
like that. Why are you asking me these, these are very strange
questions.

She writes something. She ticks two columns. Finds the next question.

Sian   Which languages do you speak?

Jonathan   I don't really, er. I've got a bit of Italian.
Conversational Italian. I can understand French, to read it at
least. Some German words. One or two Japanese words.

She writes something. She ticks two columns. She looks up.

Sian   Japanese?

Jonathan   I used to have a Japanese girlfriend.

Sian   Did I ask you that? Did I ask you that? Did I ask you
if you've ever had a Japanese girlfriend or not?

Jonathan   No.

Sian   No I fucking didn't. So why did you tell me you once
had a Japanese girlfriend when I never expressed any interest
in where the fuck your ex-girlfriends came from or not.

Jonathan   I was trying to explain why I know some
Japanese words.

Sian   Am I not asking you enough questions in the first
place?

Jonathan   It's not that.

Sian   Did I give you permission to go on oddly tangential
random meanderings?

Jonathan   No. Please.

She writes a bit more. She finds the next question.

Sian   What was the last *Star Wars* film you watched in the cinema?

What was the last *Star Wars* film you watched in the cinema?

Jonathan   Is that one of the questions?

Sian   What was the last *Star Wars* film you watched in the cinema?

Jonathan   *The Empire Strikes Back.* I don't understand why you want to know these things.

She writes something. She ticks two columns. She finds the next question.

Sian   What's your earliest sporting memory?

Jonathan   Errr. Fuck. Watching the 1972 FA Cup Final. Between Arsenal and Leeds United. Arsenal lost. My dad had friends round to watch it. They got very drunk. These questions are stupid.

She looks at him.

They are. They're stupid. They're pointless. They're stupid, pointless questions.

She looks at him.

I just don't see the point of answering questions like these. It strikes me that the only thing you need from me is my money.

Sian   Does that help?

Jonathan   Does what help?

Sian   Considering this as being a purely financial transaction.

Jonathan   It is a purely financial transaction.

Sian   It isn't.

If anybody found out what you're about to do then you would go to jail for a very long time, Jonathan.

Jonathan   They won't find out.

Sian   Are you happy that we managed to find you a girl?

You wanted a girl, didn't you?

Girls are good. They're very loyal. I'm very loyal to Frieda.
I still ring her every night. How do you like that?

How long have you been married?

Jonathan   Is that another question?

Thirteen years.

She writes something. She ticks two columns. Finds the next question.

Sian   How old were you when you got married?

Jonathan   Twenty-nine.

She writes something. She ticks two columns. Finds the next question.

Sian   How old was Fiona?

Jonathan   Twenty-nine.

Sian *writes for longer than we've seen her write before.*

Sian   That's actually good. That counts in your favour.

Jonathan   Why?

She finds the next question.

Sian   Where did you meet her?

Jonathan   Why does it count in my favour?

Sian   Where did you meet your wife?

Jonathan   On a train.

She writes something. She ticks two columns. Finds the next question.

Sian   Saucy. Where was the train going?

Jonathan   It was going to Munich.

From Salzburg in Austria.

Sian *bursts out laughing.*

Jonathan   Why's that funny? Why are you laughing?

Sian   Were you fucking inter-railing?

I'm sorry.

Jonathan   I'd just finished my teacher training. She was a student. She was doing a master's degree in German history.

Sian   Lovely.

Jonathan   The view there's breathtaking. I asked her about the lake on the German–Austrian border. I wasn't sure which lake it was. I asked her in German. I was surprised to find out she was English. She asked me to buy her a coffee from the canteen because she didn't have any money. When we got to the canteen she changed her mind. She had a beer. They have draught beer on their trains, which took us both by surprise.

Sian *receives a text. She takes out her phone. She reads it.*

Sian   Sorry. I'm always doing that to people. Reading my texts in the middle of a conversation. It's quite rude, isn't it? It's just you were saying something unbelievably fucking dull.

That was Alain. They're through. They're on their way.

She writes something. She ticks two columns. Finds the next question.

What's your earliest memory?

He looks at her for a beat.

Jonathan   When you say 'they're through' . . .

Sian   They cleared Customs. They cleared Immigration. They didn't even interview her. Everything's fine. They should be here within the next fifteen minutes. They don't have any, you know, luggage or anything. He'll take a taxi, probably. It should be quite quick.

It takes **Jonathan** *a short time to register the implications of this.*

Jonathan   When I was three I fell into quicksand. I remember, I remember, I remember.

There is some time.

I remember that my mother had to grab my hair. We were in; I think we were in Morecambe Bay. I remember the feeling of her fingers grabbing my hair. I remember her face was serious. She didn't panic. She was calm.

Does her mother know that she's here?

Did she sell her to you? Did you buy her or did you take her?

Sian *smiles.*

Sian   What job does your father do?

Jonathan   He worked in distribution. He was the managing director of a retail distribution company. They were based in Warrington, outside Manchester.

Sian   Is he still alive?

Jonathan   No.

Sian   When did he die?

Jonathan   When I was twenty.

Sian   What about your mother?

Jonathan   She died two years ago.

Sian   And your wife's parents?

Jonathan   My wife's father's still alive. He lives in Italy.

Sian   What have you told him?

Jonathan   About . . . ?

Sian   About where your daughter came from?

Jonathan   We've told him we were looking to adopt a child from overseas.

We don't see him very often.

Sian   Is that what you told everybody?

All your memories are memories of nature, did you notice that?

I think that's true for a lot of people.

We remember nature.

I hate it. Nature. It scares the living Christ out of me. I hate the darkness. I hate the quiet.

Has she got her own room?

Jonathan   At the moment I'm not living at home. There's a room in the house where my wife is living. We put that to one side for her.

Sian   Have you decorated it?

Jonathan   No.

Sian   Well, you better be fucking quick about it. Better get those ladders out, Jonathan! Sort out a quick lick of paint. A few posters. Get her a stereo. Girls like music.

What school will she go to?

Jonathan   I spoke to the school where I used to teach. I told them that we were looking to adopt. They told me that I could have a place for her there.

Sian   You'll need to pay for her medical coverage. I'm afraid you can't be completely confident about the NHS any more.

Jonathan   Stephen gave us the name of three doctors who don't live too far away from us.

Sian   For the time being it might be worthwhile getting some diamorphine for her. Getting a, what, a supply? A back-up supply. Yes?

Jonathan   That shouldn't be a problem.

Sian   Because fuck me on a horse, the withdrawal from that shit is a right proper pain in the arse and no mistake.

You'll need to be very careful about her diet. She'll need quite a regulated supply of carbohydrates for a while. She can eat rice like it's going out of fashion. You should watch that. She should just drink water for a while. No juices, you know? You should make sure she has plenty of vegetables.

Jonathan I think we'd do that anyway.

Sian I fucking bet you would.

And it'll take her a while to get used to moving about. She won't be very used to moving her legs much.

Jonathan Have you done this before?

Sian Ha.

Jonathan Have you done this before in this country?

Sian Can I tell you the one thing I always want to ask and I never really do?

Is why the fuck people want to raise a child in the first place?

This world.

Some of the places I've been to for my work, you would not believe.

I go to places where people tell me I shouldn't really go.

There are parts of the Ivory Coast. The Itury region in the Democratic Republic of the Congo. Port-au-Prince in Haiti. Kyrgyzstan. Some of the back streets of the major cities of Latin America.

I like to have a bit of a look.

Her phone goes. She answers it.

Oui. Oui. Si. Bien. Bientôt.

She hangs up.

Where are your car keys?

He looks at her. Passes her his car keys.

Where's the money?

Jonathan *and* **Sian** (*together*) In a bag in the boot.

She laughs.

Sian I guessed that.

Wait here.

She leaves.

He waits. He doesn't know if he can sit down or not. He very tentatively takes his hand off the table. He flexes his fingers. He looks at his hand as though it belongs to an entirely different person. For a brief time he seems completely outside his own body.

She returns. She is carrying a holdall. She puts it on the table.

She opens it.

She takes out several bundles of cash. They are wrapped and marked in banking envelopes.

She counts them. She says nothing.

After a while she looks at him.

She leaves again. She takes the bag with her.

She comes back. She is holding a handgun. She aims it at **Jonathan**'s *head.*

Jonathan   What? No. No. No. Please. Please. Please don't. Please don't.

She tries to pull the trigger. It's jammed.

Sian   Fuck.

She looks at the gun. She fiddles with it.

There. That should sort it out.

She aims it at him again. He tries hysterically to stop himself from crying. He squeezes his eyes closed tight. She smiles. She lowers the gun. She puts it on the table. She goes into her pocket.

Tricked you!

That always works.

You should have seen the look on your face. It was a picture!

We're nowhere near as atomised as people wish we were, you know? It's like there are synapses. We're connected. All of us.

Just when you think we can't possibly be, you realise that we are. It's horrible.

This is her passport.

These are her papers.

Dalisay Bituin. Can you say that?

Jonathan Dalisay. Bitunin.

Sian Bituin.

Jonathan Bituin.

Sian Good.

Jonathan Dalisay Bituin.

Sian It means 'the pure stars'. She's here.

Jonathan Where?

Sian Here. She's here. She's very tired. Alain's just getting her out of the taxi.

She carefully rereads the notes she made on the clipboard. She edits them as she reads them.

Jonathan What? I –

A man in his late thirties, **Alain***, enters. He is with a nine-year-old Filipino girl,* **Dalisay Bituin***. He is holding her hand.*

He is eating a doughnut.

Alain C'est lui?

Sian Oui.

Alain Il a payé?

Sian Bien sûr. Je l'ai mis dans le coffre-fort.

Alain Bon.

He lets go of **Dalisay***'s hand. She stands there.*

Alain *goes over to the clipboard. He reads it. He finishes his doughnut. Looks up from the clipboard*

Sian   You can say hello to her if you want to.

Alain   Il attend. Le taxi.

Sian   OK.

Alain *leaves. He drops his doughnut wrapper on the floor.*

Sian *picks up the clipboard and continues to edit the notes.* **Jonathan** *approaches* **Dalisay**.

He tries to reach out to her but then retracts.

Jonathan   Hello.

Dalisay? Isn't it? That's a, er, that's a very pretty name. My name's Jonathan. Are you a bit tired? You look it. Gosh. You've come a long way, haven't you? I'm going to. I'm going to. This must all be a bit strange for you. We'll get in the – You can have a bit of a sleep in my car if you'd like. That won't be a problem. I'll put some music on. Put the heating on. You can have a bit of a nap.

I like your dress. It's very pretty.

Sian *leaves.* **Jonathan** *is a bit stunned by her departure. It takes him a while to realise he has been left alone with* **Dalisay**.

Jonathan   I don't know, er. I don't know what to say to you.

Dalisay *looks at him. She rubs her eyes. He moves towards her a little. She takes an instinctive step back. He stops.*

The two don't touch.

Sudden black.

T5

T5 was written for DryWrite Theatre Company and read by Deborah Findlay as part of their DryDance night at Camden Roundhouse on 7 July 2008.

It was performed as part of the 'Impossible Things Before Breakfast' series at the Traverse Theatre, Edinburgh, on 18 and 28 August 2010. The cast was as follows:

Woman Meg Fraser

Director Dominic Hill

The monologue received its German-language premiere at the Schauspiel Frankfurt on 16 February 2011, in a translation by Barbara Christian, and was performed by the following cast:

Woman Claude De Demo

Director Lily Sykes
Set Design Olga Ventosa Quintana
Costumes Lene Schwind
Dramaturg Nora Khuon

The monologue should be read by a woman in her thirties.

Watch me. Watch me. Watch this. Here.

It's 2.45 in the afternoon. The sun is just starting to burn through the haze of the clouds. South of Burdett Road it makes spectres of Canary Wharf and the HSBC Towers. I've completed none of the things that I needed to do today.

The hum and the trundle of the traffic still moves into town. There are schoolchildren. They shouldn't be here at this time of day. There are insane people. There are people working. There are people not working. There are mothers. With their buggies. There are a hundred thousand people here.

I have to get to the vets. I have to sort the kittens out. I have to collect the dry cleaning. I have to buy some more coffee. I have to get some ice cream for the weekend. I have to make the marinade for the lamb. I need some sugar.

I need some sugar. I need to get into the car. I need to drive to the supermarket. I need to get some more parking permits. I need to fix the radiator. I need to register to vote. I need to refill the brake fluid. I must ring my mother.

I must ring my mother. I must have a look for the holiday house. I must see about his sunglasses. I must make time to read. I must watch *Gavin and Stacey* before the Sky Plus gets too full. I must go home right now this second and collect Cassie from school.

This afternoon I'm going to do none of these things.

This afternoon I'm going to turn right instead of turning left.

This afternoon I'm going to go down into the underground.

This ain't rock and roll. This is genocide.

Every single part of every single muscle feels dangerous and endangered at exactly the same time as I head past the news kiosk and ignore the Polish immigrants there trying to thrust vacuous free newspapers into my hand. Every step I take feels in some way wrong as I shuffle past the queues of bewildered tourists still figuring out the mechanics of Oyster Card renewal. The way I move my ankle or turn my head to the side feels

fundamentally naughty as I swipe my card and turn on my
heels and head to the right to the westward bound –

This afternoon the tube is full of robots. This afternoon the
tube is full of newspaper. I can't sit down. I can't move my
eyes. I can't move my hands. I can't move my chest to breathe
because every time I try there are three hundred robots here
sat stuffed up in newspapers watching me.

They'll close the school gates. They'll take Cassie with them
back to the office.

I have the sensation of feeling every article of clothing against
my skin. Feeling where it sits and where it rises, where it folds
and where it pulls. My jumper is blue. It's cashmere. It's tight.
My shirt is silk. My skirt is longer than I normally wear.

I close my eyes as the train moves west cutting under the
ground by the bomb site of Aldgate and through the ancient
hearts of the Tower and the Temple. Skirting past the river by
Embankment its movement starts to flow. And somebody told
me one time that between Westminster and St James the train
runs directly beneath the Houses of Parliament. Is that right?
Are you sure that's right? Does that sound right to you? They
said if you took a bomb on a train beneath St James and
Westminster – Can that – ? I'm sorry. I think there's been a
mistake. I think somebody's made a mistake.

By this time they'll have rung home. There'll have been no
answer. They'll ring my sister. My sister will go and pick her
up. My sister will lie to her with effortless playful ease. She
likes my sister's house. They have better things at my sister's
house. She can play with her cousin's old toys. They can get
the old toy box out.

Her cousin, my niece, is thirteen years old now. I swear
sometimes she can see it in my eyes.

I won't lie to you, baby. It's mainly a physical thing. This
feeling that I've got for you, baby. It makes me want to sing.

Changing trains at Hammersmith my chest fills up with the energy of oxygen. Fresh air hits me with a terrifying clarity and makes me very, very much want to ring back home.

I have three bars on my phone here. I have seven unread text messages. I have four messages in my voicemail. I have twelve missed calls.

It seems to take several weeks for a Piccadilly Line train to Heathrow to arrive. When it does arrive though, I surprise all of the people gathered on the platform there by carelessly throwing my phone under the oncoming wheels of the train. The driver blinks and glances in my direction with a look of distracted panic. He stops the train to let us all on as normal.

He was sixteen years old. Three boys came upon him in the playground not far from my house. It was the end of a school day. We were on our way home. One of them pushed him to the ground. One of them kicked him eight times hard in the head. One of them appeared to punch him repeatedly in the upper thigh. I only found his name out later. I only found out his age after talking to the police for four hours. I told Cassie to look at the canal. Look. Look, Cassie. There are ducks. Can you see the Mummy Duck? And all the little babies, Cassie? Can you see them Cassie? Look at the water.

By the time the tube moves above the ground and west of Acton Town it is clear that all of the remaining passengers carry heavy luggage. Many of them dress in inappropriate pastel colours. Several of them are wearing sunglasses.

There's an Asian woman staring at me. She has four bags which I think must be the same weight as her if not actually the same size. All of her bags are on wheels.

Everybody's bag nowadays is on wheels.

Momentarily I wonder at the wonder of the wheel.

And the Mercy Seat is waiting. And I think my head is burning. And in a way I'm hoping to be done with all the consequence

and truth. An eye for an eye and a tooth for a tooth. And
anyway I –

When Cassie's sixteen she'll be heading to sixth form. When
Cassie's sixteen she'll be bored shitless of me. When Cassie's
sixteen she'll be using the pill. When Cassie's sixteen she'll be
stealing my make-up. When Cassie's sixteen she'll be borrowing
the car. When Cassie's sixteen she'll have had her heart
broken and held a boy's broken heart like a bird in her hand
and wondered what it feels like to squeeze.

His leg twitched and shook and raged for only the shortest of
times. It sounded like he was struggling for breath. I stood
exactly where I was. I don't think he saw me. I'm fairly certain
now that he didn't see me. The boys ran off across Grove
Road and towards the estates on the other side of our street.

My husband had to take his glasses off as he rubbed his
eyes. My husband had to put his glasses back on to stare at
me like that. He asked me again and again when I went over.
At exactly what stage did I go over? At exactly what stage did
I go over to make sure? At exactly what stage did I go over to
make sure he was all right? Did I go over to make sure he was
all right?

I didn't just – You didn't just – I didn't just – You didn't
just – I didn't just – You didn't just – Did you just stand there?
Did you just leave? Did you just walk away?

He wrote to his lover one time, my husband, that even when
she wasn't in our house, even when he hadn't seen her for
days he could smell her on his hands. The smell of her on his
skin would just come to him.

Tonight. Oh your hair is beautiful. Tonight. Make it right.

Her Britannic Majesty's Secretary of State requests and
requires in the Name of Her Majesty all those whom it may
concern to allow the bearer to pass freely without let or
hindrance and to afford the bearer such assistance and
protection as may be necessary.

I stood in my back garden all afternoon as the afternoon passed by into night and wondered what it felt like to cut through the skin into muscle and whether when forcing it like that you felt the tip bump against the thigh bone. Is it like boning a chicken thigh, do you think? Or cutting the heavy bone of a fish in half to cook two sides of the fish separately perhaps?

I get out at the station at Terminal Five and the rush and the chrome and the glass and the size and the sound and the air and the roar and the space and the space and the space and the swell and the oil and the roof and the light and the water and space and the space and the size and the space feels like nothing I've ever quite known.

I have no idea what time it is. I have no idea where my husband is now. I have no idea what Cassie is doing right now at this second. She's wearing a little blue stripy top and little blue denim shorts over blue and white tights. And her hair needs four hair clips sometimes nowadays just to keep it in one place.

I can't do this. I don't think.

Calling out around the world are you ready for a brand new beat? Summer's here and the time is right for dancing in the street.

I don't have a ticket. I don't know how much money is left in my bank account. I don't have the slightest idea any more where I'd like to be.

Excuse me, madam? Can I help you, madam? Have you come to the right place? Are you looking to purchase a ticket, madam?

The woman on the other side of the counter is making a series of noises to me that I don't understand.

I'm half inclined to walk away. I can't. I stand quite stuck to the ground. I watch everything unfold as it happens right in front of me under the sunshine of the playground at the back of the field on the other side of Grove Road from the estates across the road from my house.

I think about what Cassie will be like when she's his age and I feel the surge and the movement of blood running through my veins like a river. When you smoke a cigarette for the first time in years it drains all your blood away from your face. And this is a bit like that.

I keep a close watch on this heart of mine. I keep my eyes wide open all the time.

I find to my astonishment that after a while people stop looking at me. I find to my astonishment that after a while people move around me as though I'm not really there. I find to my further astonishment that after a while my feet start to lift from the ground.

I swear to God I'm doing nothing to encourage or cause or contribute to this in any way. I swear to God that it's not my fault. I swear to God I wish it hadn't happened in the first place. And yet . . .

It starts with my heels raising themselves on to the balls of my toes. And then the balls of the toes leaving me standing right on the toes' very tips. And then my tiptoes start to lift off the ground too. At first it's less than an inch. And then it rises to maybe six inches. It rises further quite quickly to a couple of feet.

After the briefest of time small children begin to be able to move underneath me. I can see behind the car rental counters and the counters for local hotel information. I can see the tops of people's luggage. I can see what the check-in staff at the fast-track baggage drop are having for their lunch.

After a minute or two I'm several yards in the air.

If I move my legs it's like treading water.

I can see the world with a clarity I never even dreamed of before. And I go higher and I go higher and I go higher. Underneath me I can watch all the pastel-coloured sunglasses wearers hurrying this way and that way. It took them a lot longer to get off the tube than I did. Maybe they got off at the wrong terminal. They need to change their money. They need to buy their travellers' cheques.

I can watch all the Asian women with enormous suitcases from up here too and the police with machine guns and the courier drivers with their bored anonymous exhausted signs.

I can fly above the border control and fly above the areas that mark out the differences between arrivals and departures. I can see all the exotic spiced sandwich-makers from here (there are more exotic sandwiches being sold in this terminal than have ever been sold in one place at one time before). I can see the Passport Control staff and the people handing out clear plastic bags for toiletries below a hundred millilitres and the people making coffee and the people selling newspapers and the flight engineers and the baggage carriers and the cabin crew and the businessmen removing their laptops and the girls who have never been to the United Kingdom before and the unusual amount of people wearing neon yellow vests and the policemen on bicycles and the ambulance men on bicycles and the people travelling home for a wedding for the first time in years and the children who have flown north to spend time with their grandparents and the old woman who hates travelling alone now her husband has died and the CCTV cameramen and the men peering through two-way mirrors at Immigration Control and the people exchanging sterling for euros and sterling for dollars and sterling for yen and sterling for rupees and the people showcasing cars the like of which have never been seen on our cities' streets before.

I close my eyes. When I close my eyes I can smell her skin on his hands when she's not even seen him for days. I can see his leg thrashing and his chest trying very hard to breathe. I can see Cassie aged sixteen, holding a heart in her hand like a bird. I can see this. I don't know how to get down. I don't know how to get down. I don't know why I love you, but I love you. I don't know how to get down.

Methuen Drama Student Editions

Jean Anouilh *Antigone* • John Arden *Serjeant Musgrave's Dance*
Alan Ayckbourn *Confusions* • Aphra Behn *The Rover* • Edward Bond
Lear • *Saved* • Bertolt Brecht *The Caucasian Chalk Circle* • *Fear and
Misery in the Third Reich* • *The Good Person of Szechwan* • *Life of Galileo* •
Mother Courage and her Children• *The Resistible Rise of Arturo Ui* • *The
Threepenny Opera* • Anton Chekhov *The Cherry Orchard* • *The Seagull* •
Three Sisters • *Uncle Vanya* • Caryl Churchill *Serious Money* • *Top Girls*
• Shelagh Delaney *A Taste of Honey* • Euripides *Elektra* • *Medea*•
Dario Fo *Accidental Death of an Anarchist* • Michael Frayn *Copenhagen*
• John Galsworthy *Strife* • Nikolai Gogol *The Government Inspector* •
Robert Holman *Across Oka* • Henrik Ibsen *A Doll's House* • *Ghosts*•
Hedda Gabler • Charlotte Keatley *My Mother Said I Never Should* •
Bernard Kops *Dreams of Anne Frank* • Federico García Lorca *Blood
Wedding* • *Doña Rosita the Spinster* (bilingual edition) •*The House of
Bernarda Alba* • (bilingual edition)• *Yerma* (bilingual edition)• David
Mamet *Glengarry Glen Ross* • *Oleanna* • Patrick Marber *Closer* • John
Marston *Malcontent* • Martin McDonagh *The Lieutenant of Inishmore* •
Joe Orton *Loot* • Luigi Pirandello *Six Characters in Search of an Author*
• Mark Ravenhill *Shopping and F***ing* • Willy Russell *Blood Brothers*
• *Educating Rita* • Sophocles *Antigone* • *Oedipus the King* • Wole
Soyinka *Death and the King's Horseman* • Shelagh Stephenson *The
Memory of Water* • August Strindberg *Miss Julie* • J. M. Synge *The
Playboy of the Western World* • Theatre Workshop *Oh What a Lovely
War* Timberlake Wertenbaker *Our Country's Good* • Arnold Wesker
The Merchant • Oscar Wilde *The Importance of Being Earnest* •
Tennessee Williams *A Streetcar Named Desire* • *The Glass Menagerie*

Methuen Drama Modern Plays

include work by

Edward Albee
Jean Anouilh
John Arden
Margaretta D'Arcy
Peter Barnes
Sebastian Barry
Brendan Behan
Dermot Bolger
Edward Bond
Bertolt Brecht
Howard Brenton
Anthony Burgess
Simon Burke
Jim Cartwright
Caryl Churchill
Complicite
Noël Coward
Lucinda Coxon
Sarah Daniels
Nick Darke
Nick Dear
Shelagh Delaney
David Edgar
David Eldridge
Dario Fo
Michael Frayn
John Godber
Paul Godfrey
David Greig
John Guare
Peter Handke
David Harrower
Jonathan Harvey
Iain Heggie
Declan Hughes
Terry Johnson
Sarah Kane
Charlotte Keatley
Barrie Keeffe

Howard Korder
Robert Lepage
Doug Lucie
Martin McDonagh
John McGrath
Terrence McNally
David Mamet
Patrick Marber
Arthur Miller
Mtwa, Ngema & Simon
Tom Murphy
Phyllis Nagy
Peter Nichols
Sean O'Brien
Joseph O'Connor
Joe Orton
Louise Page
Joe Penhall
Luigi Pirandello
Stephen Poliakoff
Franca Rame
Mark Ravenhill
Philip Ridley
Reginald Rose
Willy Russell
Jean-Paul Sartre
Sam Shepard
Wole Soyinka
Simon Stephens
Shelagh Stephenson
Peter Straughan
C. P. Taylor
Theatre Workshop
Sue Townsend
Judy Upton
Timberlake Wertenbaker
Roy Williams
Snoo Wilson
Victoria Wood

Methuen Drama Modern Classics

Jean Anouilh *Antigone* • Brendan Behan *The Hostage* • Robert Bolt *A Man for All Seasons* • Edward Bond *Saved* • Bertolt Brecht *The Caucasian Chalk Circle* • *Fear and Misery in the Third Reich* • *The Good Person of Szechwan* • *Life of Galileo* • *The Messingkauf Dialogues* • *Mother Courage and Her Children* • *Mr Puntila and His Man Matti* • *The Resistible Rise of Arturo Ui* • *Rise and Fall of the City of Mahagonny* • *The Threepenny Opera* • Jim Cartwright *Road* • *Two & Bed* • Caryl Churchill *Serious Money* • *Top Girls* • Noël Coward *Blithe Spirit* • *Hay Fever* • *Present Laughter* • *Private Lives* • *The Vortex* • Shelagh Delaney *A Taste of Honey* • Dario Fo *Accidental Death of an Anarchist* • Michael Frayn *Copenhagen* • Lorraine Hansberry *A Raisin in the Sun* • Jonathan Harvey *Beautiful Thing* • David Mamet *Glengarry Glen Ross* • *Oleanna* • *Speed-the-Plow* • Patrick Marber *Closer* • *Dealer's Choice* • Arthur Miller *Broken Glass* • Percy Mtwa, Mbongeni Ngema, Barney Simon *Woza Albert!* • Joe Orton *Entertaining Mr Sloane* • *Loot* • *What the Butler Saw* • Mark Ravenhill *Shopping and F***ing* • Willy Russell *Blood Brothers* • *Educating Rita* • *Stags and Hens* • *Our Day Out* • Jean-Paul Sartre *Crime Passionnel* • Wole Soyinka • *Death and the King's Horseman* • Theatre Workshop *Oh, What a Lovely War* • Frank Wedekind • *Spring Awakening* • Timberlake Wertenbaker *Our Country's Good*

For a complete catalogue
of Methuen Drama titles
write to:

Methuen Drama
Bloomsbury Publishing Plc
36 Soho Square
London W1D 3QY

or you can visit our website at
www.methuendrama.com